AYOADE
ON TOP

A Voyage
(through a Film)
in a Book
(about a Journey)

RICHARD AYOADE

faber

First published in the UK in 2019
by Faber & Faber Limited
Bloomsbury House
74–77 Great Russell Street
London WC1B 3DA

This paperback edition published in 2020

First published in the USA in 2019

Typeset by Ian Bahrami
Printed in the UK by CPI Group (UK) Ltd, Croydon, CR0 4YY

A CIP record for this book
is available from the British Library

ISBN 978–0–571–33914–3

FSC
www.fsc.org
MIX
Paper from
responsible sources
FSC® C020471

2 4 6 8 10 9 7 5 3

Contents

PART SIX: A RAPID DESCENT

View from the Top (USA)

Released 21 March 2003

Directed by Bruno Barreto
Produced by Brad Grey, Matthew Baer and
Bobby Cohen
Written by Eric Wald
Starring Gwyneth Paltrow, Christina Applegate,
Mark Ruffalo, Candice Bergen, Joshua Malina,
Kelly Preston, Rob Lowe and Mike Myers
Music by Theodore Shapiro and Deborah Lurie
Cinematography by Affonso Beato
Edited by Christopher Greenbury, Ray Hubley
and Charles Ireland

PART ONE:
APPROACH

Clearing the Runway

On behalf of myself and the entire Ayoade Team, welcome to *Ayoade on Top*. If you were one of the dozens of people who bought (and perhaps opened) our previous offering, *The Grip of Film*, thanks for your returning custom. *Grip*, penned by the pamphleteer, taco apologist and women's rights denier Gordy LaSure, was a tough road to swallow.

Whereas that book/road essayed to be a survey of films *in general* (if by 'general' you mean homoerotic action films from the mid-to-late eighties), this book is about one film *in particular*: a 2003 cabin crew dramedy starring Gwyneth Paltrow called *View from the Top*. And this very particular film, like all exemplars of the cinematic arts, concerns a journey.

But this book is not just a book about a movie about a journey, it's also a book about *my/our* journey with that movie about a journey, a journey soundtracked by the sweet soft-rock sounds of Journey.* Or, to be precise, this book concerns *multiple* Journeys. The Journey of The Book, the Journey of The Film, the Journey of Us,

---

* Stadium mainstays to this day.

3

i.e. Me, the Journey of the band Journey and (perhaps least importantly) the Journey of You. Our destination? Well, let's just say you won't find it on any map . . . Our travel time? Unknown.* The in-flight entertainment? I guess that depends on your capacity to withstand pernickety prose in a quasi-literary sub-genre that's hard to define, let alone shelve.

It's a journey that will take us from Peckham to Paris by way of Nevada and other places we don't care about. It's a journey deep within, in a way that's respectful and non-invasive; a journey for which we will all pay a heavy price, even if you've waited for the smaller paperback edition.

We regret to inform you that no hot meal will be provided: the publishers won't commit to the catering costs.**

After three brutal years at flight academy, the captain is both within his rights and overqualified to turn on the 'Fasten Seat Belt' sign. If you haven't already done so, please stow your carry-on luggage, whether emotional or actual, underneath the seat in front of you or in an overhead bin. And please do stow it. Don't just bung it in, or stuff it in, or ram it in. Stow it, like you'd stow something in your own home, or in an Edwardian novel.

* But not long: this ain't *Anna Karenina*, aka *Madame Bovary* XL. #InYourFaceTolstoy.
** The Nazis at Waterstones won't put hotplates next to the tills.

Please also make sure your seat is back and that the folding trays are in their full upright position. Because it's not the crash that'll kill you, it's the trays.

We remind you that this is a non-smoking book. If this book starts to smoke, it means you are on fire. Ask a non-vengeful colleague to assist.

We encourage you to read this book in the lavatory, its natural habitat. But tampering with the book or lavatory in any way is an offence to the author. When finished, please stow the book back safely in its display case.

The doors to this book have now been secured, and we will shortly taxi* to our runway, if we take 'runway' to mean 'further introductory passages', 'taxi' to mean inelegantly trundle like a chest freezer on a roller skate, and 'doors' to have no real relevance within this piece of high-wire idiomatic world building.

Thank you for choosing *Ayoade on Top*. We are aware you have many other entertainment** options and we would like to thank you for choosing this one. We know that you could be ploughing through the media on your thumbstick, belittling a spouse by contrasting their career with that of a contemporary or gorging (guilt-free!) on some wind-dried puffin. But instead you've

* When did 'taxi' become a verb?
** The word 'entertainment' sits somewhat uncomfortably within the Ayoadean multiverse . . .

chosen to buy (or at least not immediately re-gift) this book, and that makes us particularly #humble. You are almost too aware that there are many other, better books on the market, yet despite the fact that you may well go to your grave without reading *In Search of Lost Time* by Proust, *Don Quixote* by Cervantes or *My Booky Wook* by Russell Brand, some combination of kindness, misplaced optimism and laziness has led you to this one. We thank you and hope your mounting regret doesn't metabolise into a more lasting resentment.

A Brief Message from Our Captain

There are moments in your life when things change for ever. It could be the discovery of an unexpectedly pleasant dipping sauce, a night-time visit from your financial team or a ticketed white-collar grudge match.

For me, it was a movie.

I'll never forget the day in June, or maybe it was March, in either 2013 or 2014, when I opened up my laptop, attached the external DVD player with a (male to male) USB cable to the 'puter port, swabbed the screen with a lemon-fresh (and moist!) towelette, removed a shop-bought DVD from its slightly chipped Amaray case, checked for marks and scuffs that may have resulted from in-transit disc slippage, attended to said marks and scuffs with a sober squirt of CleanSafe fluid* and the use

---

* Can't say enough good things about this product. Specially formulated to work effectively on DVDs/CDs, I won't use anything else on my collection. And believe me, I've tried everything, from milk to the hot breath of a cat. The coating of any DVD/CD is delicate, so you don't want to use anything overly abrasive. (I once saw a former friend try to remove some (of his?) semen from a CD with kitchen towel: I don't think I've ever slapped a paper product out of someone's hand so fast!) Using low-conductivity fluid (and, BTW, CleanSafe's conductivity is approx. 17 per cent that of water) ensures that the risk of static, magnetic or electrical damage is substantially reduced, allowing you to get the sleep

of my (somewhat careworn!) rotating microfibre cleaning cloth, placed the DVD in the external (top-loading)
disc drive, waited for the DVD icon to appear on the
desktop, pulled up an open-source, cross-platform media
player like VLC or RealPlayer, dragged the icon across
and, with the carelessness of young middle age, double-
tapped the trackpad.

Let's pull out wide.

I'm lying on my bed, laptop perched regally on a pil-
low that in turn was resting on my meaty quads, not only
for extra height, but also to stop the heat of the computer
from causing my thick thighs/private delta to mist and/
or puddle.

Venetian blinds hoisted high, window open, sound on
MAX, faint smell of synthetic lemon in my nostrils, the
room is provocatively bright.* The glare on this screen is

---

you need. CleanSafe claims to leave 'a smooth, non-sticky, acoustical
and optical pure nano layer so as to protect the disc', as well as offering
'excellent anti-static protection to slow the build-up of static dust'. If
you're looking for a contrary opinion, call your boys at Radio 4, cos this
brother ain't got no beef. It's an outstanding product that, at last, puts
safety front and centre in the cleaning process. All housed, might I say, in
a very attractive, slimline, lightweight bottle that's small enough to keep
in your pocket, tucked into your belt or, if the situation demands it, your
anus. My only fear is that I'll run out! (As if! I have fifty bottles in my
panic room!!!)

* With age comes fatigue/self-hatred (one of my few remaining urges is for
the oblivion of slumber), so closing the curtains is fatal. If a cloud obscures
the sun for too long, I'll wake up an hour later, looking for someone to

unreal. My eye-drops commingle the hitherto divergent feelings of burning and wetness.

I'm trying to breathe like I learnt from that vlog. At least I think I am. Should breathing sound like the bongos? Can you breathe to excess? I should rewatch.

So it turns out I've been breathing the wrong way for three years. Can I ever get that lost oxygen back? Is that why I'm always tired? Why I find it hard to focus? I find myself on YouTube, watching a compilation of Extreme Slap Bass. I close the curtains a smidge.

I wake up in the same room, only now it's dark. This Slap Bass Comp has been thumping for 7h 06min. Had a dream I was in Level 42.* My thumb was as big as a mountain.

It's 3 a.m.

I'll tank up on toast and see if I can push through till dawn.

Why am I here?

Shhh! The film's about to start.

But before we roll titles, let's grab us a slice of background.

---

blame. And there's only so many times you can phone people to ask them why they let you fall asleep. Especially if, hitherto, they had no way of contacting you or knowing that the tide was coming in that fast.
* Proof that great funk pop *can* come from the Isle of Wight.

Before We Depart

2003 was a clustered year at the box office. Vying along-side the soon-to-be-seminal *Kangaroo Jack*, *Bruce Almighty* and *How to Lose a Guy in 10 Days* were the comedies *Just Married*, *Dickie Roberts: Former Child Star* and *Charlie's Angels: Full Throttle*. More intellectually challenging fare, like *Bad Boys II*, *Jeepers Creepers 2* and *Scary Movie 3*, duked it out with future classics *Freddy vs Jason* and *The Matrix Reloaded*, while pastoral works like *The Lord of the Rings: The Return of the King* and *Pirates of the Caribbean: The Curse of the Black Pearl* crushed it both commercially and financially.

Perhaps it was the sheer quality of 2003's output that meant a smaller film like Bruno Barreto's *View from the Top* (budgeted at a mere $30 million) struggled to make its mark. It was too subtle, too provocative, too counter-cultural for its time. Here was a film that dared a pre-Trump America to believe in itself again, with its exhortation to work like hell, play like hell and take responsibility like hell, even when it wasn't really your fault. This was an unashamedly cerebral film starring that icon of third-wave feminism, Gwyneth Paltrow, in an English-language dramedy that charts the highs and lows of Donna Jensen, a Small-Town Girl from the Wrong Side of the Tracks, as she pursues her dream of becoming an air stewardess. Here was a protest against the narrative of victimhood that has come to pervade today's Complaint Culture. If you want to succeed, the film bravely asserts, put on a short skirt and go into the service industry! It won't be long before you're picked out for even greater things, like higher-paid work within the service industry! Because if you're hot, you'll reach the top! And if you're a little heavy or have a squinty eye, maybe you can work behind the scenes, where you won't spook anyone.

This book (in its own modest way) hopes to rehabilitate a work that Paltrow has disowned as a 'money job', as opposed to more 'meaningful' films in which she gets to play emotionally brittle mathematicians. As a prominent star of screens both small and large, I know only too well the impulse to play down one's more populist gifts. It's far easier to feign interest in 'independent' cinema (which will soon be filmed and viewed solely on its natural 'platform': the smartphone) than to shine light (perhaps using the 'torch' function on that same smartphone) on those parts of ourselves that are vulnerable, hard to find and (frequently) raw. It's better to hide in the comfort of the snot-cry, the drunken scream and the hollow-eyed oh-the-humanity-shower-slide than to commit to

11

the nuances of a comic montage showing small improvements over time.

Top is a rare, breathless work of honesty, directness and integrity, a film that celebrates capitalism in all its victimless glory, and one I can imagine Donald Trump himself half watching on his private jet's gold-plated flat screen, while his other puffy eye scans the cabin for fresh young prey.

PART TWO:
DEPARTURES

A View from the Pre-Titles: Emotional Baggage

The image is unsteady. Colourful. A young girl looks at us. She is Caucasian: blonde hair, blue eyes. Hitler would have been thrilled. We feel an uber-surge of maxi-relief. This isn't going to be some 'worthy' virtue-signalling film about social issues/justice. This is the opening frame of a Super 8 montage. This is going to be a normal, nostalgic film about attractive white people who get everything they want.

The girl is a child actress called Chelsey Cole. Cole smiles, but the smile doesn't convince. It's thin. And not just because you suspect that the director, off camera, is shouting, 'Chelsey, is there any way you can make the smile a little less thin?' There's something else. Perhaps Cole already knows that this, the part of Young Donna, will be her best role. Post-*Top*, she will only manage to put in a playful performance as Poinsettia in 2003's fantasy dramedy *A Light in the Forest*, before giving her swansong as 'Young Jennifer'* in Vin Crease's sensitive

* Old Jennifer (credited as 'Jennifer') is played by Cheryl Dent, whom you will recall from writer/director Nick Gaitatjis's 2006 dramedy *Gettin' It* – a post-*American Pie* boner movie in which a teenage boy is falsely

2005 psychological horror dramedy *Slaughter House of the Rising Sun*.

But before we can dwell on why Cole quit this business called show, Young Donna places an eye mask over her own face. Is it a coincidence that the mask looks very much like the sleep mask we might place over our own (broken) faces on long-haul flights or if we're losing an argument? Is this girl, like we the audience, about to enter a dreamscape? A land of unconscious flight? Like Gloucester from *King Lear*, will she see *better* without eyes? Or will she lose her way?

The camera pulls back to reveal that Young Donna is surrounded by four other children of similar age. They hesitantly start to spin Young Donna around, as per their child minders' instructions. It would seem that this is the precursor to a popular child's game, like pin the tail on the donkey. But look closer. There is no board. There is no donkey. There is no tail. Endlessly spinning the blindfolded Young Donna *is* the game. These children have nothing to do except rotate. The thought appals. How long will this hazing ritual last?

A non-diegetic intrusion. A voice. Female.

'Every story has to start somewhere.'

---

rumoured to have an atypically large sex organ. The film explores the comic (and poignant) ramifications of this misunderstanding. It's another sensitively handled piece about the urge to connect.

Fair enough. No argument with that. It's a bloody reasonable thing to say. In fact, throughout what follows, the film's sustained, masterful use of first-person narration obviates the need for potentially protracted scenes in which important character motivation might be revealed visually. Instead the narrator, Old Donna – or, as she's credited, 'Donna' (Gwyneth Paltrow) – simply *tells* us what subtext, if any, is *not* revealed by cutaways of signs and newspapers, expository flashbacks and the cast's often varied facial expressions. If something about a character's motivation or a particular incident is unclear, don't worry; Old Donna will *explain* what's going on. This is brutally direct filmmaking. And I welcome it.*

Then, with characteristic confidence, director Bruno Barreto cuts to a banner saying, 'Happy Birthday'. How refreshing that he trusts us to put two and two together. Like Lubitsch before him, Barreto makes his audience work for their fun! Whose birthday *is* it? We will have to wait to find out. This is drama: Expectation vs the Controlled Release of Information!**

Sensing our disorientation, Old Donna, in her thorough

---

* If Orson Welles had had this gift, *Citizen Kane* might still be remembered today. He could have clarified that weird ending with a simple line of VO, saying something like: 'And that's when I, Citizen Kane, realised how much I loved sleds.'
** I'd pay to see that wrestling match!

and continuing voice-over, tells us we're in Silver Springs, Nevada.* We are then both told *and* shown** that Donna's Mom (Robyn Peterson) is an ex-showgirl – 'emphasis on the "ex"' (so presumably she's really, really stopped being a showgirl) – while Young Donna's father (name unknown, actor uncredited) is only 'there for the beer'. However, the *mise en scène* makes it look like the father has brought his own brew. If he has – and the film does not dwell on this moment – his presence could not be causally linked to the presence of the cold gold:*** presumably he could consume that can in a car park of his choosing. If loudmouth juice**** was indeed provided, it begs the question of why Donna's Mom – seemingly estranged from this uncredited actor – would allot any (limited!) funds supposedly for kids' party items (stream-ers, balloons, etc.) to the good stuff.***** Perhaps there were some suds****** for attending adults, but then

* Up until 1940, Nevada was the least populated state in America and as dry as your momma's tongue, until its libertarian laws (which relaxed restrictions on prostitution, gambling, liquor and divorce) saw the population, and the flourishing of its heart, increase concomitantly.
** An *in camera* rebuff to the moronic maxim 'Show, don't tell'. It's 'Show *and* tell', and we know this from *school*: if you 'show' and *don't* 'tell', your teachers do not hail your visual virtuosity; they mention the lapse in your daybook.
*** Beer.
**** Ibid.
***** Ibid.
****** Ibid.

18

why is the father being uniquely vilified? If the implication is that Donna's Mom is dropping dollar money on neck oil* rather than necessary party items, perhaps it is *she* who should be held to account! Thus, we have a work that is near ceaseless in its capacity to provoke, throwing up question after question, urging us to begin a dialogue with the film in its first few frames. This is a narrative that will resist easy (or even logical) answers.**

Barreto then treats us to an artful top shot of a small table holding up a birthday cake, like some kind of trestle Atlas. Again, Barreto trusts us to fill in the gaps: someone must have placed that cake on the table since it was brought out of the trailer by Donna's Mom in shot 3. But who? Answer: *it doesn't matter*. That's why Barreto didn't show it.

The cake is a four-candler, yet Young Donna looks significantly older. Perhaps her parents' poverty has led them to conserve/hoard candles? Therefore, one candle for every two years? Donna = eight?

A lighter enters the frame. A female hand attempts to light one of the candles. There's a spark but no flame. A deft foreshadowing of a failed romance to come.

* Beer.
** For example, one is left to try to work out which friend/family member is shooting and editing all this costly Super 8 film footage, given the fact that Donna's Mom can only afford to live in a trailer.

19

Lord, this onion's layered.

A wide-ish two-shot of Donna's Mom and Young Donna depicts the mounting frustration on Donna's Mom's face. The dialogue is suggested through gesture, the arch of an eyebrow and, in due course, gurning. 'How come this lighter won't produce sufficient flame to light these candles?' Donna's Mom seems to be saying. 'And now of all times! I'm being thwarted, and I don't like it!'

When we return to the same top shot of the birthday cake, an off-camera gust blows some napkins and paper cups through the frame. We know almost immediately that it's windy. *Just through image.*

Conclusion? Lighting these candles is going to be no picnic. And it's windy! What kind of fun can you have in wind?

By way of an answer, we see Donna's Mom and Three Other Women (uncredited) forming an impromptu chorus line, while singing 'Happy Birthday, Donna', finally clearing up the mystery of whose birthday it is. It's Young Donna's. Of that much we can be close to certain.

We are low-angle, over the shoulder of an unidentified sleeveless boy (it must be windy *and* hot). A dejected Young Donna looks at the cake. It now has six candles on it. This seems like a more realistic age for her. Has there has been an off-camera discussion between Young Donna and Donna's Mom that perhaps they could stretch to another couple of candles to better reflect her actual age?

A dejected Young Donna holds on to a red balloon, an echo of Albert Lamorisse's 1956 multi-award-winning Balloon and Boy dramedy *The Red Balloon*, in which a lonely youngster, estranged from his peers and family, befriends a heavily anthropomorphised inflatable. For a while it's all high jinks and skipping, but when the crimson bladder is fatally punctured by some Parisian urchins, the indefatigable dirigible calls on his colleagues from the balloon world to form a giant cluster blimp and Zeppelin this young beta male to ... well, we don't know. The film ends with the tiny squit sailing up into the sky with no real game plan. It's all very well for the music to swell, but what kind of landing is this kid going to have? Plus, he's only in shorts. That's charming at ground level, but impractically chilly at altitude.

The camera zooms in to a closer shot of Young Donna. She lets go of the balloon, which flies out of frame. Children are often upset when they lose a balloon. But not Young Donna. She doesn't care. (But note: it is a helium balloon, so some money has been spent on this party. Those things don't inflate themselves. Either Donna's Mom has her own canister or she's gone to a local toy store. *Quand même*, palm has intersected with dollar.)

Loathe to leave any subtext unexcavated, Old Donna gives us an auditory tap on the scapula. She never got to blow out her candles (although why didn't they just light them inside the trailer – unless it was even windier inside?), but she does remember wishing to get as far away from Silver Springs as poss.

So, at the tender age of either four or six, depending on which insert shot of the cake we are to believe, Young Donna sets her heart on *international* relocation. But why? Is it the lack of structure to the spinning game? Is it her fear of sudden breeze? (Because that's not specific to Nevada. Try wearing a fedora in Felixstowe.)

I thought Young Donna's party looked pretty good. There was a banner. There was cake. People attended. That's better than my last birthday. That's better than any of my birthdays. Plus, when you're six, who cares where you live? Children are still excited by puddles. To them, a low wall is a mountain range. They are fascinated, for prolonged periods of time, by bubbles. And they don't even care if they are the ones *blowing* the bubbles. They will chase bubbles *blown by others*. And you can buy children off with tiny amounts of money. They feel that one pound is sufficient compensation for the loss of a tooth. They think glitter comes from unicorns. They don't care about topography. They don't worry about the difficulty of getting glitter out of carpets. And they certainly don't care about *neighbourhoods*.

When I was six, I didn't even know it was possible to *be* anywhere else. All I did was stay in the car. My parents were always in the car, going to places, getting out of the car at those places and asking me to stay in the car until they got back from those places. But they needn't have asked. Where else would I go? It never occurred to me to leave the car. The only reason I wasn't still in bed was because I was told it was time to get out of bed and get in the car. As an only child, I never learned to conspire, no one showed me how to rebel. I simply did not know *how* to transgress. I did everything I was told. My first words were, 'Will that be all for today?'

It wasn't until I was in my late teens that I realised I didn't have to wear the exact things my mother told me to. Finally, I could stop dressing like a cabin boy. I opted for a look which said, 'Youth is wasted on me!' – baggy corduroy, tucked-in checked shirts and tweed jackets. I looked like my own supply teacher.

In John Milton's Fall of Man dramedy *Paradise Lost*, Satan muses on his exile from heaven:

> The mind is its own place, and in it self
> Can make a Heav'n of Hell, a Hell of Heav'n.
> What matter where, if I be still the same,

And what I should be, all but less then he
Whom Thunder hath made greater?

In short, he's had a shocker, but he's trying to look on the bright side. Getting chucked out of heaven is a profound bummer. This isn't getting frozen out by Matt from sales because you didn't invite him to your *Great British Bake Off*-themed fortieth; this is God asking you to leave His kingdom, and by all accounts He's not a Huge One for self-doubt. There is no verse saying, 'And lo, God felt that, on second thoughts, He'd been a bit hasty, so He said, "Adam, mate, at the end of the day it's just a bit of fruit. It's no biggie. I felt a bit mugged off by your missus, I'd been working a six-day week, I'm a little bit tired and emotional, we're all new to this game, come back to the garden and we can thrash it out over a couple of tins."'

For the Evil One, it's not where you are, it's who you're with, and as long as he's bouncing with his boys Belial and Beelzebub, he doesn't give a cloven hoof about the locale. Conversely, your man could be maxin' in Mustique, but if the Lord of the Flies is on the adjacent lounger, your man may as well be in a bay of turd. Or Ibiza.

Young Donna could take a leaf out of Satan's skin-bound book, try to get some perspective and stop with the sad eyes. But instead she seeks solace in the sky.

The balloon lifts away and disappears. The frame widens past its Super 8 square shape to become the widescreen of our feature presentation, a change of texture and ratio as bold as anything in the woefully self-conscious *Wizard of Oz* or Andrei Tarkovsky's slumber party *Stalker* (which I thought would be a slasher film, not a challenge to my desire to remain conscious).

The title comes up, over a darkening sky:

VIEW FROM THE TOP.

A whole world has been built; a backstory has been painted in but a few brushstrokes; sixty seconds have slipped by in what seems like mere minutes.

But before we press on, a little backstory of my own . . .

A View from the Road: Happy Eating

From the age of six, my family, all nuclear three of us, lived in the rightly renowned district of Martlesham Heath, a sophisticated enclave about twelve klicks east of Ipswich nestled 'neath the sheltering shadow of one of British Telecom's most glorious industrial parks. It was far away from the distracting bustle of society, yet still close enough to the A12 that you could forever hear its roar in your dreams. Every day, when we drove to school or to the nearest shop for fresh earplugs, we would pass our local Happy Eater, branch number 89 of the franchise.

For younger readers, or older readers who are middle-class and up, the Happy Eater chain was created to rival Little Chef, which, until then, was the only national network of roadside restaurants in Britain. Before, if you were out on a long car trip and wanted something to eat, you just stopped your car in the middle of the motorway, popped on your hazards and ate your sliced white straight from the foil.

I became obsessed with that Happy Eater. I would beg my parents to let me eat there. They always refused. 'What do you want to eat out for?' my parents would ask. 'There's food in the house. Also, why are you bothering us? Can't you see we're watching the news?' When my parents weren't watching the news, they were either waiting to watch the news or recovering from watching the news. The news confirmed their feeling that things were terrible everywhere, and there was nothing anyone could do about it apart from keep abreast of developments. I've avoided the news ever since.

The menus of Chef and Eater were comparable – rubbery eggs, sturdy burgers, wet chips and luminous bean juice – but the Eater had a secret weapon: animal-themed outdoor playgrounds, allowing the next gen to let off some steam, while the passing lorries let off a little carbon monoxide. Mum could pour herself another tepid coffee, while Dad could open up the newspaper and wrap his peepers round some well-earned tits.*

Visually, I always felt that Eater had the edge over Chef. The latter's logo was restricted to red and white (predating the White Stripes by a generation – I still can't listen to 'Seven Nation Army' without wanting to order the crumbed fish fillet), showing a small figure – was he a child or was he far away? – a ghostly, gurning, deflated Michelin man–boy, hubristically holding aloft a hot plate, from which plumed three graphically precise 'S's of steam,

* Up until January 2015, tits were still regarded as 'news'.

his rictus concealing the pain of his burning flesh, while his foreground hand reached towards us in what was intended to be a gesture of welcome but looked more like an attempt to retain his balance, as if the tightrope beneath his tiny feet had been airbrushed out. In more recent times, the steaming plate has been removed from the image, yet the figure's stance remains unchanged, making it seem as if, just prior to his immortalisation in signage, the dish had been swiped by a disgruntled sous-chef. Instead of looking like a figure ready to serve, the Little Chef now looked like someone who was going to press you into an unsolicited bear hug, one that would include several pats on the back and possibly a wet one on the neck.

By contrast, Eater's iconic logo was subversive and simultaneously iconoclastic: a red, round-faced punk in profile, spiked tuft atop the crown; the eye a single black dot in a white crescent moon; mouth brazenly agape; a disembodied hand pointing to the back of the throat, a memorably unmoored mitt that created the impression of *trajectory*, as if it was going to end up in the mouth *itself*, making it impossible to know for sure whether the 'Eater' in question was indeed 'happy' or rather a bulimic trying to put on a brave face, albeit a cartoon one. Was this figure desperately trying to disgorge, or was it so loud in this raucous roadhouse that all communication would have to be done by mime?

The 'Happy Eater' legend underneath the figure was in a futuristic font, a little like the one used in the movie *Rollerball*, and, in my imagination at least, it spoke of the coming apocalypse: that after the Big One, the Eater would be where we'd scrap it out with the other survivors for a slimy slab of meatanium, washed down with a barely warm quart of guzzleade and a septic shot of vodkron.

But what both Chef and Eater shared was that subtle squirt of *je ne sais quoi*, something that set them apart from my previous dining experiences: table service. *De temps en temps*, I would salt some crackers al fresco with the Maths Camp Massive or sink some sherbet while out strolling with one of my imaginary acquaintances, but in an Eater or Chef you were witnessing the outworking of a master–servant relationship as old as the Mesopotamians (but this time with air conditioning at selected outlets). By feting my *naissance* at an Eater, I would move up the dominance hierarchy from Boy Held Down and Farted On to International Sophisticate Laughing at Prior Subjugation with New-Found Friends. 'Was this the boy whose head we used to flush down the toilet?' my oppressors would ask. 'This bon viveur so suavely swirling his Thousand Island dressing with a carrot baton?'

After months of petitioning, my exhausted parents agreed to take me to our local Eater for my birthday, though they would not honour a previous verbal commitment to rent me a tuxedo. My father was short (he wasn't the full Pesci, but he barely needed to duck to get in a car), so I was able to walk fairly safely in the jacket I'd borrowed from him, which, on my still shorter frame, looked like a tweed dressing gown. It went without saying that 'what with the crazy prices of eating out', festivities would need to be bare bones: no presents, we'd reuse last year's hats, and instead of a cake we would segment a Mr Kipling's when we got back to base. Also, no other guests unless they were of independent means, i.e. no guests. *Tant pis*: this would be the best birthday of all time/space – an intimate table *à trois*, partially reheated food, sophisticated conversation across the generational divide and easy access to the A12.

But when we arrived, the edifice of my Eater Dreams turned to Eater Shit. The playground had been commandeered by some rough boys, who though young (five and under), were not about to budge from that giant giraffe's mouth, so I was denied the carcinogenic cardio I so desperately craved.

I had neglected to bring any reading material, and my dad was looking at some lovely news, leaving me with no option but to flick through the *Daily Mail*. But before I could start feeling subconsciously oppressed by Brussels, my dad stood up. He was leaving, and seeing as he had the keys to the car, so was I. My mother would have to let that watery coffee go to waste. The roundabout was too busy to leave safely by foot.

My father found it hard to cope with waiting in general, and at restaurants in particular. He felt that the food should be at the table before he was. That's why we never went out to eat. Why would they entice you with pictures of food that they hadn't even started to make? That would be like going to the newsagent and waiting for the journalists to finish writing the captions. Who had that much time to spare? He had news to watch, letters of complaint to compose, feet to put up, half-moon glasses to misplace. He had no option but to ripcord.

'But it's my birthday,' I protested.

'Is that', he said, 'my fault?' If we went now, we could catch Nicholas Witchell settling into his chair on the *Six O'Clock News* to tell us which depressing things had occurred most recently. The party, and my birthday, were over.

Why this deviation from the central thrust? What's a roadside eatery got to do with *View from the Top*? In a word: empathy. I too know what it's like to have a disappointing birthday party. I too know the terror of unexpected gusts, be they environmental or alimentary. I too know what it's like to want to leave somewhere. My main problem is knowing where to go once I've left.

In short, Donna Jensen, *c'est moi.*

At the time of going to print, Happy Eater is no more, its menus barely googleable, its premises refurbished into Costa Expresses.*

An era has passed, as all eras must. What is left to say, except the answer to the question, 'What do you call Gloria Estefan vomiting in a taxi?'

Sic transit gloria.

---

* A collection of rapidly furring nozzles protruding from unmanned cargo crates.

A View of the Flight Attendant
as a Young Woman

Bruno Barreto's camera tilts down from the sky to a tableau of the adult Donna Jensen (Gwyneth Paltrow) sitting in front of her mother's trailer. The elegance of the camera move almost threatens to distract us from its symbolism. Barreto, working from an Eric Wald screenplay, contrasts the still-relevant concepts of 'up' and 'down' with the more esoteric notions of 'front' and 'behind' by directly tying them to physical, *observable* forms. *Up there* (sky) lie dreams. *Down here* (land) lies reality. Donna is sitting on her bottom (*behind*) in *front* of a trailer. *Behind* her, lying on *his behind* (on a *soiled* couch), seemingly asleep, is her mom's fourth husband, Pete. This is the bedrock of great directing – translating *ideas* into images. Donna needs to get off her ass and reach for the sky, or she'll end up here for ever!

Then, with typical economy, Barreto suggests that Pete (David Hayward) may be drunk (liquid is often a sign of danger in this film) by directing his actor to turn unsteadily onto his side, thus knocking over an empty beer bottle, as well as a plate of recently proffered burgers. As Donna's Mom clears up the mess, issuing reproaches under her breath, Donna looks on ruefully. Perhaps this isn't the first time she has seen this tableau . . .

Donna turns her head back towards the lens and gazes out (note the *direction* – she wants 'out' of Silver Springs), her expression unmistakeably sad or bored or perhaps tired. But Barreto is not so foolish as to rely on the communicative capacity of the human face! He cleverly reinforces the moment with a clarifying line of voice-over: 'I still had my mind on a different life, beyond Silver Springs.'

Cut to Donna 'making out' with 'high-school quarterback' Tommy Boulay (Marc Blucas) during an American football match, underneath some stadium-style tiered seating. Here, in contrast to when we last saw her, Donna seems animated and full of zest. In fact, she tells us in voice-over that Boulay was 'a great kisser', but this potentially rich seam is not developed. It's a rare misstep and, in fact, makes me wonder (1) *why* Boulay's such a good kisser, and (2) why is Donna *assessing Boulay's performance in what is meant to be an intimate act of non-judgement*? In any case, the result is that I'm briefly bounced out of the film, and a strange sadness drifts through my body.

However, Tommy Boulay looks as if his mind is elsewhere. It is unclear whether his evident worry is due to the exploratory force of Donna's tongue, ambivalence over their relationship or whether he's due back on the field. In voice-over, Donna tells us that she knew that 'together they were going places'. References to motion abound in Donna's commentary: here, the film seems to ask whether 'going places' is the same as 'going to a place'. The first is a perpetual cycle. Sisyphus is going places, it's just that the route is quite up and down.

An assistant manager at Big Lots, Boulay uses 'his pull' to get Donna a job in the baggage department. Big Lots, Inc. is a large-scale American retail company, incorporated in the state of Ohio, with over 1,400 outlets in forty-eight states. They are essentially department stores, specialising in 'closed-out' or overstocked merchandise, and while it has a proud history stretching back to 1967, when Consolidated Stores Corporation was formed in Ohio by Sol Shenk, we get the impression that Donna Jensen's dreams extend beyond working in Big Lots. But what are we meant to feel about the other employees of Big Lots? Do their lives not have value? Are they not, as the film posits, 'going places'? Cinema helps us to remember that although we all have the right to shine, some of us must shine in the background, out of focus, and not too brightly. It's also to the film's credit that the motif of Donna working in the baggage department (while working through her own 'baggage') never feels arch, but merely thematically on point. Interestingly, there is no indication as to whether Donna targeted Boulay in order to get the job or whether the job opportunity was a stroke of serendipity, post-'hook-up'.

The idea of Paltrow working in retail might sound like a sour note from a less seasoned throat than Barreto's. Barreto brought us the nun-murder dramedy *One Tough Cop*, a film that cast Stephen Baldwin (who alternates between a pout that says 'thinking is hard' and the smile of a post-poo baby basking in gooey relief) as an Italian American. A director brave enough to do this is just the man to cast Paltrow as a girl from a trailer park. A born contrarian, Barreto takes a clichéd crime scene in which a cop asks, 'What kind of animal would do this?' and, instead of subverting it, surprises you by not subverting it at all.

Had *One Tough Cop* been directed by a lesser man, he might not have had the courage to include the line 'And then my flashlight takes a shit on me' without having someone laugh straight after it, but Barreto lets it stand, and as a result gives the words terrifying power. Maybe, we think, this policeman's flashlight actually did shit on him. No wonder he's so rattled. If his flashlight took a shit on him, he would be forgiven for wondering what other improbable things might take a shit on him in the short to medium term. For such a man, sleep would be a memory. Another director might say, 'No, we can't have a scene every five minutes in which the Hot-Tempered

Cop is dragged screaming from a fight by the Even-Tempered Cop. No, we can't do all our exposition in bars. No, we can't have the top brass call the protagonist the Best Damn Cop on the Force. No, we can't give his best buddy a gambling problem. No, we can't have a scene where someone is confronted over unpaid parking fines with the line, "You've got parking tickets up the ass." No, we can't have his childhood friend go into organised crime.' Not Barreto. Barreto says 'Yes' to all these things. It is in the unvaried repetition of familiar motifs that Barreto's originality lies.

At first glance, Paltrow looks like she wouldn't set foot in Big Lots even if it were the only viable place to shelter from acid rain. She hates conventional retail so much she's set up her own company to filter out anything non-bespoke and named it after what Stephen Baldwin's smile seems to be wallowing in.* For Paltrow to enter an establishment without being offered ionised cucumber water is unthinkable. But it is Barreto's job to make us think the unthinkable. His camera cranes down (high/low vs up/down) as Donna extols the virtues of a particular piece of luggage to a customer ('nylon twill with DuPont protective coating'). 'This is the bag you use when you fly?' asks the customer, somewhat provocatively. Donna

* Goop.

37

is forced to admit she's never been on an aeroplane, but if she ever gets to go on one, this is the bag she'd like to take. It's a moving exchange. It subtly reminds us that, thus far at least, her ambition to leave Silver Springs remains unfulfilled. But shortly two key events will propel her skywards.

A View of Goop

On 5 October 2018, after a lawsuit instigated by California's consumer protection office, Gwyneth Paltrow's lifestyle website Goop was ordered to pay $145,000 for making unscientific claims about vaginal eggs. One of the most surprising things about this verdict is that, by logical inference, it must be possible to make scientific claims about vaginal eggs. It is also surprising that someone would want to pretend that there is such a thing as a vaginal egg. Vaginal eggs are the result of taking the name of a body part and placing it next to the name of a breakfast item. Vaginal eggs are no more real to me than penis toast or anal pancakes. As my mother would always say to me, nothing that can hatch belongs in your vagina.

According to *Business Insider UK*, 'The eggs are each about the size of a narrow ping-pong ball – around 1.2 inches wide and 1.7 inches tall* (a bit smaller than the colourful, plastic kind at an Easter hunt).'

Two questions press:

* Scientific fact: this would be like having a slightly larger version of Donald Trump's penis inside you all the time.

Why did they think we couldn't imagine an egg without first thinking of a ping-pong ball?

Why are people playing table tennis during Easter-egg hunts?

Undeterred, *Business Insider UK* continues: 'There are two varieties: a rose quartz crotch egg that costs $55, and a jade version for $66.'

If I were to put something in my vagina, I would like the feeling that I'd paid the extra $11.

The 'staffers' on the Goop website tell me that the egg is 'pre-drilled for string add-on' (they recommend using unwaxed dental floss, but I suppose you could decide to attach a yo-yo) and that the item is 'non-returnable'. But surely it should only be non-returnable if you've inserted it into your vagina. I would suggest that most consumers presume that once they've inserted goods into their vagina, those goods are non-returnable, whether it be a moth strip, a travel kettle or a fidget spinner. Once it's gone in, it's a keeper.

Business Insider UK, still the natural go-to magazine for those of us still passionately disinterested in the exteriority of UK commerce, cites the views of Jen Gunter, a California-based obstetrician and gynaecologist who just happens to have a name that sounds like a Nazi folk heroine. She says that if you want to build vaginal strength (me please!), then there are specially designed vaginal weights for that. Not only are pelvic-floor muscles not *meant* to contract for several hours in a row, jade is porous, making it an ideal place to house bacteria. And as my mother always said, 'The last thing my vagina needs is more bacteria.'

Goop claimed its jade and rose quartz eggs could balance hormones and regulate menstrual cycles, 'among other things'. The key word here is 'could'. Goop is not saying that these eggs can do these things. That is not the Goop way. Goop says these things 'could' balance hormones and regulate menstrual cycles. They could also 'not' do these things, and Goop accepts that. Some of the 'among other things' these particular eggs might do is cause discomfort or infection or anger at having bought them.

But Goop is more than a peddler of intimate pro-late spheroids. It is, in its own words, 'a modern life-style brand', its website offering 'cutting-edge wellness advice from doctors, vetted travel recommendations, and a curated shop of clean beauty, fashion, and home.' How 'wellness' differs from 'being well' is unclear. If you were to ask a Goop 'staffer' how she was, would she say, 'Well, thanks,' or would she say, 'I have wellness'? We don't know, but whatever she says, she's going to remain super-centred.

Goop is the online manifestation of the party into which the Blue-Collar Hero walks; a party where everything is strangely clean, where uptight sophistos sip complex cocktails; a party where an Alpha Yuppie says to the Blue-Collar Hero, 'Nice boots, did the hobo mind when you stole them?', forcing the hero to ask the Alpha Yuppie if he wants to repeat that, so the Alpha Yuppie says, 'Are you deaf as well as dumb?' while his Beta Yuppie cohorts laugh and high-five in the background, so the Alpha Yuppie modulates his voice into a low hiss and impugns the Blue-Collar Hero's position in the linear intrasex ranking system with a salty remark about the latter's mother, whereupon the Blue-Collar Hero puts out his cigarette in the Alpha Yuppie's complex cocktail, causing the Beta Yuppies to go 'ooh' and the Alpha Yuppie to say, 'Shut up, you chicken shits. Hold my Armani jacket – I don't want to get blood on it when I break this motherfucker's nose,' but as soon as he turns, he's met with a swift uppercut to his pinstriped chest. The Blue-Collar Hero leans over the Alpha Yuppie's felled form and says, 'You talk too much,' before riding off on his motorbike with the Peach-Skinned Prom Queen and giving her sweet boom-boom on a weirdly clean hay bale, because all these uptight broads basically just want to be shown What's What by a Real Man with a single strategic smear of bike oil on his vest.

But these days, the Peach-Skinned Prom Queen doesn't want to leave the party. She's 'catered' the party herself with farm-to-table organic food. Her business partner and best friend is DJing. The party's carbon neutral. Ellen is there. She and Portia can't believe how many delicious nuts and pulses there are to try. Why would the Peach-Skinned Prom Queen leave with someone who doesn't care enough about the planet to offer her an eco-friendly transportation option? If he was a Real Man, why would he want their unconceived children to breathe in those fumes?

Goop celebrates Real Men, but Goop also celebrates self-love.

'When a trip to the sex store left product designer Peder Wikstrom disenchanted, he decided it was time to disrupt the industry.' I've never visited a 'sex store', but I'm surprised that anyone who has would go with the expectation of enchantment. The USP of a sex store is not the renewal of one's faith in the sublimity of the human soul. Nevertheless, Peder Wikstrom's spirit had sagged unduly, so he called his former co-worker Mattias Hulting, who was no doubt wondering why you couldn't get a really lovingly made butt plug any more, and the pair created 'four playful, sexy vibrators, bringing not just their sleek design sense, but also a sense of humor into what's often an overly-serious, less-than-aesthetic product category'.

I always find this idea of people bringing 'cheekiness' to *anything*, let alone erotic implements, one of the most off-putting ideas imaginable. I don't know that you can insert anything into yourself in a 'quirky' manner. If you're going to insert, insert, but don't kid yourself that you can insert something that has inverted commas around it – those things are going to hit the sides.

Peder, who I hope never labelled any of his files with his first name, asked a thousand women about their sexual fantasies, and then named the vibrators after the most popular ones: the Millionaire, the Frenchman, the Tennis Coach and the Fireman. The first to sell out was the Millionaire. Nothing is more sensual than solvency.

'They're also super-silent, battery-powered, [and] waterproof,' allowing you to keep wanking even when you're being held hostage in an underwater cage, miles away from a viable power outlet.

Goop is a place where you can buy a 'kid calming mist' (a cross between a humidifier and a riot cannon) and a 'psychic vampire repellent protection mist'. The latter is to be sprayed 'around the aura to protect from psychic attack and emotional harm'. Which is crackers. How can you spray something around your aura when you are already *within* your aura? You would have to get some-one else to spray it on your aura. But who can you trust? Everyone's psychically attacking you!

Goop is a place where everyone's skin is not merely 'glowing', it's 'glowy'. I don't know the difference, except that I think 'glowy' skin maybe looks wet. Glistening. As if all that expensive moisturiser hasn't sunk in yet; sort of, if you'll permit me, goop-y.

Goop is a place where you can 'reboot your Fall', even if a boot caused your fall in the first place.

Goop is where Gwyneth Paltrow (or GP, as she's acronym'd) lives. On the cover of the Goop book, *Goop Clean Beauty*,* GP stands on a beach. She wears no shoes. Even when she's standing, she's exfoliating (naturally). GP wears a dress as white as her teeth. But unlike her teeth, the dress is almost see-through. It's the kind of dress you can only wear if you know it's unlikely you'll have to hold anything yourself. She's massively relaxed. And centred. She has centredness, wellness and mindfulness, along with other 'nesses' we probably won't even hear about until the next newsletter.

For Donna Jensen to even dream of such a woman would be beyond her capacity. GP's life is Olympian, a true *View from the Top*. A view that only one superspecial old soul with youthful glow-y skin can command.

---

* GP is not the author of this book, but she does provide the foreword. Getting your foreword game tight is one of the most important things you can do as a prominent media figure. You don't have time to write a book. You're a prominent media figure. But you sure as hell have time to say that this book you haven't written is the kind of book you would have written if you weren't so busy living a life that would make the tedious task of organising extended passages of words a fatal distraction.

We who want to be clean, we who want to be beautiful, we who wanted the Millionaire but had to make do with the Tennis Coach can either fill our virtual baskets or, from afar, pooh-pooh Goop's lofty mound. But our sticks and stones don't hurt GP. They don't even reach. We don't have the upper-body strength. We don't have the right peer-rated nutritionists. We don't have the laser-like mindful focus that might have tackled our destabilising back fat before it started to define us. We crumple onto the silty shore, lethargic from the build-up of toxins within us, and we cry the tears of the ordinary.

Perhaps the reason *Top* is so touching is that it speaks of a time when we could imagine Paltrow aspiring to be better than average, rather than better than the world itself.

A View of Escape

Barreto's camera frames a locker. We see three iterations of the name 'Donna':

1. Within a pink heart.
2. On a sparkly background surrounded by stars.
3. On the background of a sparkling star.

Conclusion?

This could well be Donna's locker. And Donna is someone who wants to shine. But as the camera pans down, we see that's not all she wants to do. Various aspirational messages are affixed to the surface:

1. Teamwork is not a solo sport.
2. Go hard or go home.
3. When the going gets tough, the tough get going.*
4. The ship moves when everyone pulls an oar.

---

* A saying which Billy Ocean turned into a truly uplifting song. Note: another of his hits, 'Get Outta My Dreams, Get into My Car', is one of the few pop songs which (correctly) contends that without reliable transportation, there can be no romance.

5. Kindness is contagious.

6. There is no 'I' in 'team'.

Two things are apparent. Firstly, Donna Jensen has no fear of cliché. Secondly, at the end of the day, Donna Jensen is a pack animal. She believes in the value of the collective over the individual. She prizes loyalty, joint responsibility and – in a way that's truly refreshing – literalism.

As the camera finishes its tilt, a male hand enters the frame, using a novelty magnet to affix an envelope bearing the legend 'Donna' to the locker door.

We cut wide to reveal Donna Jensen walking into what looks like a small changing room. We see that the locker is one of a row, and that the hand belongs to Tommy 'The Tongue' Boulay. Behind Boulay's shoulder is a small sink, the kind of sink you and I might wash our hands in, or our private parts. But Boulay's hands are covered in blood. Bad blood.* The kind of blood Taylor Swift hates.

Jensen's first line of the scene – 'I caught you' – is, like so many in the film, loaded. Boulay is reluctant to let her read the contents of the envelope and secretes it in his back pocket. Donna flirtatiously retrieves the item

* One of the great pop-based rebuttals to the ludicrous notion of forgiveness.

48

and opens it. It's a birthday card. But when she reads the message contained within, her face crumples, like a drained can of Fanta under a Cuban heel. Barreto resists the temptation to cut to one of his statement insert shots, and instead lets this moment play on Paltrow's harrowed face. Tommy Boulay is breaking up with Donna Jensen. Donna can't believe that Boulay would break off intimacies with a birthday card. Displaying a disingenuousness that will guarantee he no longer participates in the narrative, Boulay flippantly says that it's because they don't make 'breaking-up cards'.

Evil, thy name is Boulay.

We know by now that Donna takes birthdays very seriously: they're an opportunity for her to take stock of her dreams, get rid of any balloons that might be holding her back and use her internal monologue to tell us what she wants to do next. So the news that Boulay and his new paramour are leaving to pursue business opportunities in Arizona could be enough to crush her, were she made of lesser stuff.

Donna balefully asks whether Boulay's undisclosed co-conspirator is Linda from Lawn Chairs, before Boulay admits that it's Brenda in Barbecues. This exchange feels like a rare misstep and seems to veer from the reality so carefully established thus far. While the badinage is undoubtedly witty (this is an Eric Wald screenplay),

49

are we to believe that people are only hired at Big Lots for their alliterative potential? Why, then, isn't Donna in Dinnerware? Or at the Denim Bar? Also, unless Boulay's been held back for reasons of academic under-performance, a high-school quarterback is unlikely to be older than seventeen or eighteen – pretty young to land an assistant-manager gig. So why is he so impatient to move on? Donna is clearly much older, so her restlessness is understandable. Indeed, it seems odd that given their obvious age difference, she would expect him to commit so soon. Did they ever talk about their relationship goals together, or is she falling into a paradigm of passivity, per-haps reflecting the helplessness of her windy childhood?

Then Boulay takes the subtext from just below the surface and hauls it up on deck. He tells Donna that she's just a small-town girl, that she belongs here, and that business is business. It is one of the strengths of the screenplay that if ever there's a chance of thematic ambiguity, someone will verbally intervene and, bluntly, restate the theme. The phrase 'business is business' will haunt us later. It's a phrase that's hard to refute, much like the phrase 'genocide is genocide', but the trauma of this rejection will lead Donna to harden up and focus on her own 'business'. Business that will take her far away from Silver Springs, business that will take her to business class and beyond.

But in the short term, Donna goes to a bar.

The Depressed Protagonist at Rock Bottom in a Bar is a potentially overused motif, but it's familiar for a reason. It's a cave-like setting, in which the wounded animal that is (Wo)Man retreats, regroups and reassesses, often in the company of a sympathetic supporting character who likes to obsessively dry-wipe glassware.

It speaks to the archetypal story of Jonah and the Whale. And if you've ever been to a Wetherspoons, you'll know exactly what it feels like to be in a whale's mouth. Except no one could stay in a Wetherspoons for three days and get out alive, let alone prophesy the destruction of Nineveh. The floor in many Wetherspoons is even stickier than a giant tongue (and the smell somewhat more brine-y), but being in a 'movie bar' allows an opportunity that's rare inside a whale: the chance for the camera to slowly move towards you while you have a revelatory thought.

In this scene, the thought arrives via a television screen. Donna sees a talk show featuring Sally Weston (Candice Bergen), an ex-flight-attendant-turned-lifestyle-guru who is promoting her book, *My Life in the Sky*. She is described as a little girl from Texas who went on to become the most famous flight attendant in the world. We do not pause to ask, 'How did she become famous?' We take the statement on trust, just like the child who has to trust us when we tell him or her we're too tired to go in goal at the moment and that it would be even more fun for him or her to keep kicking the ball against the wall. Were we to think about whether we know of *any* famous flight attendants, we might rob ourselves of the opportunity to enjoy the narrative.

There *are* famous people who *used* to be flight attendants, but the most likely way to become famous *as* a flight attendant is to hijack the plane. And it was a plane hijack that stopped *View from the Top* from being released in 2001. The studio heads felt that in the aftermath of the most destructive terrorist attack to occur on US soil, a film making light of being a flight attendant would be inappropriate. Such was their urge to honour the victims of 9/11 that they didn't feel it would be respectful to recoup their investment until the fuss had died down. They also took the opportunity to return to the editing room and revisit the film in the light of the tragedy. Perhaps it was the moving images of firefighters and civilians joining together to sift through the wreckage and attend to the injured that gave them the idea to include a pre-credits blooper reel, as a tribute to what was lost.

Meanwhile, back on the fake TV talk show, Sally Weston starts to say some things that are uncannily pertinent to Donna's situation. People told Weston that *she* was nothing and that *she* would never amount to anything. Then she realised that her dreams were not waiting 'down there' (gesture), they were waiting 'up there' (gesture). As well as positing the notion that dreams have heights, Weston is insistent that you can be whatever you want, regardless of background. But, she adds for reasons that are hard to fathom, you have to start right now.

Weston is calling on Donna (and us) to believe that complete personal transformation is an act of will. Here the film seems to be in dialogue with the work of Terrence Malick and his perennial examination of a post-exilic world in which Nature vies with Grace. What can (Wo) Man achieve through 'works' versus what is 'given'? Do we choose to love (as the T-shirts tell us), or *must* we love? If we have not love, have we life? You'd certainly need to send fewer Christmas cards. In *Top*, as in Malick's (lesser) *Tree of Life*, 'works' is symbolised by Career, 'grace' by Family. This is Donna Jensen's Struggle. Though in many ways the film is a struggle in its own right.

'You have to start now.' The question hangs in the air, as challenging as a debate on *Channel 4 News*. Donna stands up, walks towards the bar and steps into one of Barreto's loving close-ups.

'But how?!' she asks, helpfully making exterior a thought that acting alone might not convey. Sally Weston seems to look at Donna, and by so doing, at us. Her answer? 'You've gotta buy my book.'

We don't need to see Donna buy the book; the act of

purchase is implied when Barreto cuts to her reading it. Pure Eisenstein. A third meaning created by the juxta-position of two shots: thesis, antithesis, synthesis. Bravo, Barreto.

A flurry of telling inserts follow:

1. DONNA'S HANDS pull open a DRAWER.
2. DONNA'S HANDS pick up some clothes from the DRAWER.
3. Camera PANS to an open holdall.
4. DONNA'S HANDS zip the holdall SHUT.
5. INSERT SHOT: a newspaper on the 'CLASSIFIED' page.
6. DONNA'S HANDS toss the holdall into the OPEN trunk of a car.
7. CLOSE SHOT: DONNA'S HANDS turn KEY w/ FUN FOB in the ignition of a car.
8. DONNA'S HANDS yank down the GEAR LEVER.

It's both a great piece of filmmaking and a red-letter day for Paltrow's hand double. This dizzying montage concludes with the money shot: Donna's smiling, yet determined, face.

Her journey has begun.

A View of Journey's (Un)End(ing)

Mike DeGagne, from the website allmusic.com, contends that 'Don't Stop Believin'',* the 1981 soft-rock anthem that deftly underpins *View from the Top*'s opening scenes, contains 'one of the best opening keyboard riffs in rock'. I would argue for Van Halen's 'Jump' and, in fact, have (with Mike DeGagne himself). The exchange ended with me calling DeGagne a 'farm boy' – a reference made solely in relation to the genealogy of his name. *Gagner* is an old French word meaning 'to till' or 'cultivate', and therefore it's very likely his ancestors *were* agricultural workers. I presumed DeGagne would know that, but I now accept that the nomenclature could be 'regarded as derogative', and after a period of intense pressure from some aggressively vocal farming lobbies, I reluctantly deleted the tweet.

The version of 'Don't Stop Believin'' on *Top*'s soundtrack is not the Journey original but a new, sensitive, cost-effective rendition by John Koha from the

---

* In 2009, 'Don't Stop Believin'' became the top-selling track in iTunes history among songs not released in the twenty-first century, after featuring in *Glee*, a show that would feature Gwyneth Paltrow in a move that I always read as an intertextual reference to *Top*.

band Escape, one of the leading Journey cover bands currently active.* Although DeGagne praises Steve Perry's expansive range on the original recording, he feels that the vocals verge on overpowering, so perhaps it's just as well that the version used in the film employs the thinner, reedier, ultimately 'weaker' voice of Koha.

But while DeGagne praises the 'enticing' and 'cutting guitar work' of Neal Schon in his 'review', he also makes a reference to what he terms the band's 'adolescent adventurism' – a term so *casually* condescending that it makes me wonder whether anyone even *cares* about quality online rock writing any more. Founded by ex-members of psych-rock pioneers Santana and Frumious Bandersnatch, Journey released three albums:

---

* This from their website: 'Like Journey, Escape features five of California's top tier rock musicians. All the players have endorsement deals with major musical gear companies, including ProTools, Bognar Amps and Paul Reed Smith guitars, and several Escape members have endorsements and/or beta test with cutting-edge amp/effect manufacturer Line 6. More than one of Escape's players has played with Keith Emerson, Toto members such as Bobby Kimball and David Paich, Kelly Hansen (Foreigner lead singer), Howard Leese (Heart, Bad Company), Glenn Hughes of Deep Purple fame, 70's hit-makers Hamilton, Joe Frank & Reynolds, Stuart Smith and Joe Retta of Sweet, former AC/DC drummers Chris Slade and Simon Wright, three different *American Idol* finalists, and even former members of Journey. There is no other Tribute to Journey that has the musicianship and experience – and the ability to play and sing every note with all the subtle nuances of the original – like Escape.'

Journey, *Look into the Future* and *Next*, before recruiting singer Steve Perry in 1977, a move which displayed both humility and *maturity*. Here was a band who had the courage to say, 'Not one of us can cut it vocally, we're down a rhythm guitarist (George Tickner) and we know that (our musical prowess notwithstanding) the most communicative instrument in rock is the human voice. So let's embrace Perry's pipes and be our best selves.' This is a decision made by *adults*. Adults who, as a result of accepting that they couldn't just smoke herb, play twenty-minute guitar solos and hope to make a dollar, came to dominate the stadium-rock scene in the eighties, standing shoulder to shoulder with the likes of Foreigner and Europe. This was a band who *didn't stop believin'* in themselves. Is it any wonder that they would write such an enduring anthem?

And by using the song so prominently, *View from the Top* seems to be asking us, albeit non-diegetically and in rock form, to *bear with it*. Forget the film's poster, where no one's head seems to belong to their bodies, forget the casting of Paltrow as a blue-collar Midwesterner, forget the suspiciously clipped running time (eighty-seven minutes including bloopers, followed by both an unmotivated dance sequence and a drawn-out credit crawl), if we all just decide to *believe*, we can make it through. It's this 'groundless' belief that we should – as it were – *keep*

57

watchin' that makes the experience of *Top* so touching. Complicity is created, binding the filmmakers to us, its limited audience.

There are, of course, times when one might be wise to *stop believin'*.

Why, for example, didn't we *stop believin'* in infinite economic growth pre-2007? In early 2008, I had to accept that I could no longer keep up the payments on my south-east London garage share. It became apparent that seventeen people couldn't effectively co-own a garage. And even though none of us could afford a car, meaning that we might have been able to use it for (limited) storage, once we broke the garage down into zones based on our individual contribution to the sale price, no one could enter the (tiny) space without triggering a complex border dispute. Legal fees swallowed up our investments, and some frankly vile accusations were made both in person and online. Before we knew it, some middle-class squatters had repurposed the property and turned it into a falafel nook.

But those times – times of doubt, disorientation and white rage – are not within 'Don't Stop Believin''s mandate. 'Don't Stop Believin'' is perhaps the most potent paean to credulity in rock. Indeed, the only thing 'Don't Stop Believin'' asks of us is to *persist with our current belief*. As regards *what* we should believe, the song is silent. Journey don't care *who* we are; we could be Satanists, as long as we're consistent.

How long should we *keep believin'*? If you think Journey are going to be prescriptive about that, you don't know Journey. But the question remains. Do we maintain our 'belief' for the duration of the song, or until we lose brain function? If the former, the call to arms seems a little self-serving, as if the time for *believin'* is tethered to the track: highly convenient for a stadium-rock act with its inevitably fascistic focus (let us note that the premier pop phenomenon of recent memory was called One Direction). If the latter, the song can start to feel like a straightjacket, a manifesto for abso-lutism, and while Journey are many things, they're not absolutists. In fact, the song is as exhaustingly *relativ-ist* as it is *impractical*. In this regard, the song's *credo* reminds me of Kenny Loggins's 'Meet Me Half Way'. As well as containing what must be some of the slow-est drum fills in pop-rock history, the song announces itself as an appeal for compromise and mediation – two notions sadly absent in much of rock – before Loggins makes the entirely *un*reasonable, not to say logistically challenging, suggestion that his lover meet him halfway across the sky.

It's a verse that displays such a worrying ignorance of the limitations imposed by international airspace that you start to doubt whether Loggins is in earnest about meeting up *at all*, or whether he resides in a kind of esoteric dream world – something that would be maddening for any partner, especially one committed to building a life in common.

And yet unlike the band Journey or the man Kenny Loggins, *View from the Top* knows that beliefs change. Perhaps that's what marks the difference between an enduring work of cinema and soft rock. Donna Jensen's journey will see her core assumptions challenged and her endurance pushed to the limit, again mirroring our journey as viewers. In fact, Jensen's journey starts off with her *believin'* in a world (in the sky) that *can* belong just to her and *not* you and I. But this big-haired Icarus will modify her beliefs. As she grows, she will come to realise you can fly only so high, and if life is a lock, the key is moderation.

Addendum: the DVD extras* to *Top* include a short piece about the music used in the film, presented by Randy Spendlove.** Spendlove says *View from the Top* is about chasing your dreams, but I disagree. I think the

* The wonderfully titled 'First-Class Features'. It's good to see that the creativity that burst forth in the making of the film continued into the home release!
** The only reason I believe this is his real name is that he doesn't look like he'd be able to think it up.

film is about coming to realise that the dream that helps you be your best self is already in the centre of your own heart, if only you dare to believe (i.e. no chase required).

But how do you find the centre of your own heart?

Don't stop readin' . . .

PART THREE:
TAKING OFF

What to Expect When You're Expecting (to Fly)

'Everybody has to start somewhere.'

Perhaps the day will come when Donna Jensen's *pensées* are collected in a coffee-table book, alongside other epigrams like 'What goes up must come down' and 'Better out than in', but for now we must be content to consume them through the orifice of Barreto's camera.

Barreto shows us a dry, barren terrain. In its middle, absurdly, like something Beckett might have written if he'd had ever had the balls to come up with a plot, is a trailer. Has Donna travelled all this way to end up where she started? No. Because this trailer is an office, one that bears the legend 'Sierra Airlines', which makes it more than an office: it makes it a gateway.

During Sally Weston's TV appearance, the host asked her, 'Why flying?' It's a brilliant question, but one that Weston swerved with obfuscating new-age aphorisms. Now, that question is echoed by Roy Roby (John Polito), head of Sierra Airlines. He sits behind a cluttered desk, made to look chaotic by a conscientious art department. Sierra Airlines is a run-down service whose business motto is, according to Roby, 'Big hair, short skirts.'

I doubt that this is true, and neither does it really describe what Sierra Airlines does, i.e. no frills budget flying for half-cut businessmen. What Roby neglects to mention is that the uniforms are extremely tight. If I had to wear clothes that tight, I would have to start buying my talc wholesale.

Donna claims that two things drew her to the subtle art of the stewardess: the 'travel opportunities' and the 'excitement'. But it's hard to believe that she could find the self-affirmation and freedom of which Sally Weston speaks in commercial flight, with its pointlessly strict safety regulations, yahoo-laden cargo and increasingly tight turnaround times. Working as cabin crew (the term 'stewardess' is hopelessly dated, but we must bear in mind that *Top* was released in 2003, before feminism finally found its footing) is exceedingly demanding. One would think that only those with an unexplained fetish for blocking narrow passageways would be attracted to this role, so onerous are its duties.

I decided to look into the matter by googling 'cabin-crew conditions'. After a dispiriting two-hour Amazon detour, I found this prescient 'post'. I quote verbatim from what is, grammar-wise, the Wild West:

Our job is governed by flight time limitations. Depending on what the time is when we sign on for

66

flying duty we can fly X amount of sectors (flights) but we cannot fly more than Y amount of hours. Ranging from 9 hours to 14 hours. For ULH (Ultra Long Haul) we can augment flight time by sleeping in bunk beds on board at the rate of 2:1, so for each two hours in the bunk we can fly one hour more, or 3:1 by being provided with curtained seats. If we can fly there and back within our limit it's a turnaround. If there isn't enough time it will be a layover. Usually minimum rest is 11 hours. But due to the way schedules are made, if there is only one flight there a day we will usually stay 24 hours. Some countries will only allow an airline to fly there 3 times a week, in which case we stay either 48 or 72 hours. When we do fly ULH it is often the case that we stay 48 hours as our minimum rest has to be equal to our last flying duty, minus one hour. Some airlines operate multi-sector trips, starting off at base, flying 3, 4 or even 5 flights in a day before ending up in a city where they will get a hotel until the following day. Sounds complicated? It is!!! Sorry, could not come up with a simpler answer. :o) – theSebster.

Fact is, a commercial aeroplane is one of the most restrictive environments in the world. Want to know the difference between a commercial aeroplane and communist China? You can smoke, guff and make consensual love in communist China without fear of reproach! Once a plane is in the air, you can't even leave it! I've tried! They won't let you! You have to wait until 'they land'.

This shadowy, depersonalised, frankly militaristic 'they' (why *should* I call the pilot 'captain' – I didn't join his army) is what makes commercial air travel so Orwellian. Say you want to take a nap, what do you ordinarily do? Take off your trousers, clear a space on the floor and maybe set an alarm on your phone. Sometimes I've lain down on the pavement for a week, and no one has bothered me. People on my street know me, and they'll either hop over or take a brief detour into the road. On a plane it's all, 'Sir, you're blocking the trolley.' Don't call me 'sir' and then *tell me what to do*! Even the homeless get to sleep lying down. A squatting vagrant huddled in his hovel has more room than the 'executive' in business class. How can it be a business-class service if you don't get your own toilet? Some of the worst things I've ever smelt I've smelt after opening a business-class toilet. And I'm the one embarrassing myself?! Please. Go smell what's in the business-class toilets, and then we'll talk.

Donna, duly hired, barely has time to backcomb before encountering Christine Montgomery (Christina Applegate) and the surname-less Sherry (Kelly Preston), both equally condemned to wear uniforms that are at loggerheads with circulation. In fact, Sherry is introduced in the kind of manner ordinarily reserved for the 'bad girl' in a reform-school drama. We meet her in the staff bathroom as Donna practises saying, 'Sir, please fasten your seat belt' in the mirror. Following the sensual sound of a cistern emptying itself, Sherry slinks out of a stall, a vision in purple nylon. Any thought as to the accompanying odour is far from our minds as the camera pans up from her oddly futuristic boots.

Sherry asks if Donna is nervous, the implication being that if she too needs to void her bowels, that's totally cool. Donna flashes a smile that tells us she's either bunged up or she's dumped her load. With a knowing wink, Sherry struts to the basin, insouciantly turns on the tap and fixes Donna with a look that says, 'This is *my* toilet, and don't you forget it.' Donna watches Sherry as if to say, 'Wow, this dame sure knows her way round a toilet.' Indeed, Sherry delivers a one-woman tutorial in no-soap hand-washing. 'All you need do', the implied dialogue goes, 'is simply rinse off any visible urea and faecal matter before drying.' For this, Sherry uses a wall-mounted hand dryer. Donna watches in awe. Perhaps she's never seen one before? Maybe her school was a hand-towels-only affair. But that might be for the good. We all know that flushing a toilet can cause faecal matter to travel up to fifteen feet in the air, but what is less known (aside from who the hell has fifteen feet of air space above their toilet) is that said faecal matter can be sucked up by said hand dryers and turbo'd back onto said hands. Said faecal matter can also lodge itself in garments. That's why, when I use a public latrine, I leave my jumpsuit in the stall and walk out the way God intended.

Donna and Sherry, booted but barely suited, strut onto the airfield. Barreto establishes Donna's unease without making fun of it, finding the sweet spot between her legitimate concerns about Sierra Airlines' operational anomalies (pilots asleep in the cockpit, fuel dripping from the fuselage, black smoke billowing from the engines, etc.) and the fact that the genre (up-tempo, star-driven cabin-crew dramedy) absolutely prohibits the death of its protagonist. Barreto would be hard pressed to maintain the good-natured clip of the piece if Donna's maiden flight ended with a solemn sift for the black box, but neither must he present the poor cove as a delusional paranoiac unsuited to our sympathies.

Happily, the sequence (in which Donna both literally and figuratively takes off) is a delight. Helped by a group of committed extras, Paltrow shows any would-be thespian the exact right way to pitch comic panic. Lesser artists might be shrill. Not so Paltrow. Her refrain of 'We're going to crash' moves us with its light touch, and her frenzied run down the aisle is committed, climaxing in a close-to-camera scream that manages to be both harrowing and good-natured.

After this standout set piece, Donna finds a kindly ear in Co-Pilot Steve Bench (Rob Lowe). 'Turbulence is tough – you'll get the hang of it,' he says, sagely. And when Donna evinces doubt, he gives her the clincher: 'I'm a pilot – it's my job to know where people are going.'

It is unclear why Co-Pilot Steve thinks that his undoubted ability to successfully co-pilot a plane would be a subset of a more general omniscience. With a uniform that could be euphemised as 'snug' and a face that looks like it was made in a particle accelerator using only cheekbones and twinkles, Co-Pilot Steve's level of self-assurance is troubling, possibly sociopathic.

Curiously, we never see Co-Pilot Steve again, and it seems odd that an actor of Lowe's stature would take on such a small part. One immediately wonders whether there is a deleted Co-Pilot Steve subplot. Would he continue to speak only in the idiom of transportation? Were things to turn to the physical act of love (and with Co-Pilot Steve that possibility feels disturbingly urgent), would he, mid-embrace, say, 'You are now free to roam about the cabin?'

We don't know. But for Donna, Co-Pilot Steve's few words work. By the next scene, she has become an exemplary member of the cabin crew: negotiating orders, safety briefings and snack distribution with the ease of an old, moisturised hand.

Barreto and his scribe, Wald, are wise to omit any scenes showing *how* Donna gets better at being an air stewardess. The medium of cinema finds it almost impossible to convey the labour required to achieve excellence in a given discipline. How can a film show a lawyer mastering her craft? She carries stacks of books, she drinks coffee, she stares at books while rubbing her eyes, she eats Chinese takeaway from the carton, she lays her head on the desk in tiredness, she wakes up with an egg roll affixed to her cheek, she puts her hair up in a bun, she acquires horn-rimmed glasses, she starts wearing less revealing cardigans, she wins the case, she is rewarded by a romance with the less flashy of the two men who are sexually interested in her.

Cinema is much better at showing us the rules of a game, and then allowing us to watch people play by those rules. That's why there are so many great movies about Scrabble. Equally, sport holds the attention of millions because the rules are static. Take two people, one elevated flat surface, one lightweight white ball. It's thrilling, it's unpredictable, it's tournament table tennis, and we can't get enough of it.

As Donna moves into her imperial phase of cabin-crewing, 'I'm Not Anybody's Girl' by Kaci Battaglia plays non-diegetically. It's a moving manifesto of self-attestation, in which the titular girl rejects her former lover and strikes out on her own. The verses outline what an absolute barnacle this bloke is, and how there is nothing he can do for her that she can't do for herself, and when push very much comes to shove, this rotten blister could drop down dead and the total effect on Kaci Battaglia would = nil, the conclusion very much being that this chap can go hang for all she cares, i.e. relationship terminated, thank you very much. The last thing Kaci Battaglia needs is a man, apart from perhaps the two chaps who wrote the song. James McCollum and Jason Levine have done their bit, but as far as the coarser sex goes, that's it, with the possible exception of Joel Diamond, who produced it, and Walter Turbitt, who did additional mixing. But now that she has the song in which she sings of her independence, it's very much Kaci in the driving seat – a seat in a car that may have been made, yes, by men, but that's not the point. Like Donna, she is 'flying full speed ahead' (on the ground – ground that has been tarmacked by men most probably, but why bring that up? It's irrelevant).

VFTT, while being a resolutely *visual film*, is remarkable for the resonance of its language. Much of the voice-over can be read on one level, but often there's *another* level above that first level. Donna is literally in a plane that is flying 'ahead' at 'full speed', but the expression 'flying at full speed' might not be merely a description of the aircraft's velocity; it could be interpreted as referring to Donna *herself*. Like the plane, Donna has 'momentum'. But is she merely 'in flight' from her real problems? (Yes.)

Just as Donna's career is 'taking off', the film cleverly complicates matters, of which more in course's due.

Go Fly Yourself

In *Ways of Seeing*, John Berger writes: 'Men act and women appear. Men look at women. Women watch themselves being looked at.'

We 'see' this in commercial aviation.

The pilots (who are mostly men) remain behind a door and will only speak to us via an intercom, and then only to tell us that they're going to make various unilateral judgements. The cabin crew, who are mostly women, point, remind us how a whistle works and tell us the best thing to do if we fly into a mountain is to put our heads between our legs.

Berger goes on to write: 'This determines not only most relations between men and women but also the relation of women to themselves. The surveyor of woman in herself is male: the surveyed is female. Thus she turns herself into an object of vision: a sight.'

But by this point, Berger was obviously losing focus. How can you 'survey' something inside of you? It's dark in there, and pretty gloopy. And women clearly 'act' as well as 'appear'. In fact, Gwyneth Paltrow's job *is* to appear to act and to make appearances e.g. at a Goop pop-up or in front of large groups of nerds, appearing to care about being in a comic-book film. Acting is the shop window; the shop itself is highly marked-up aspirational bullshit. It's high-end bullshit, but it's still bullshit. But to be fair to Berger, we all bifurcate ourselves. When I buy *Finnegans Wake* by James Joyce, the acquisitive part of me is buying it for the deluded part of me that thinks I'll read it one day, while the archivist part of me keeps it on a shelf with all the other books I haven't read, so that one day it can present a logistical problem to those who survive me.

The stewardess also 'acts'. She has to hyper-heat meals until they form an impregnably encrusted superstructure. The pilot also 'appears'. He knows he looks fly in those aviators, wheeling that wheelie bag. He doesn't *need* those epaulettes. Neither do Coldplay. They *like* those epaulettes.

Airlines have long adopted the stewardess as an emblem of allure. In 1971, the US-based National Airlines took out an advertisement featuring a stewardess looking straight at the lens. The type above reads, 'Hi, I'm Cheryl. Fly me.' What the advert doesn't make clear is how that would be possible. Cheryl appears to have none of the qualities required that would allow her to travel unaided through the atmosphere without touching the ground, let alone if she were saddled with an overweight and horny businessman. Unless they're tucked discreetly out of sight, there is no indication in the photo that Cheryl has wings or fins. Presuming she is no less heavy than air, we know that for Cheryl to achieve any kind of aerodynamic lift she'd need a propeller or a jet engine. And given there is no outward indication that Cheryl is an airbound insect, her only option for flight would be if she were launched ballistically as a human cannonball. And that can only take you so far. The current record was set in 2011, when David 'the Bullet' Smith Jr travelled just over 59 metres before landing in a net. And he comes from good projectile stock. His father, David 'Cannonball' Smith Sr, is rumoured to have travelled 61 metres at the Steele County Free Fair in Owatonna, Minnesota, but the distance was never verified, and the date never specified. In Minnesota, one imagines, days can drag. Perhaps that's why Smith Sr took to blasting himself as far away from the arid sod as he could get and encouraged his son to do the same.

But I'm not entirely sure that this is what we're meant to think when Cheryl says, 'I'm Cheryl. Fly me.' Cheryl probably isn't inviting the prospective traveller to join her in a compressed air cannon, to be violently expelled into a net in front of some semi-interested agricultural specialists. So what is Cheryl suggesting? Surely Cheryl isn't being presented as an eroticised canvas onto which the male traveller is meant to project his own propulsive thrust? That would make the airline her pimp. Does National think that the consumer is going to be so gripped by the illusory prospect of stratospheric congress that he's going to book a flight he wouldn't have taken anyway? Is his wife going to wonder, 'How come all these needless flights all of a sudden?' Also, unless National are thinking that, post-ad, they'll only be accepting one passenger at a time, is this an invitation to a *ménage*? Will robes and lotions be provided? Or will you have to bring your own lube?

And in the event of an emergency, is this consumer going to insist on remaining in his sexual fantasy? As Cheryl guides him through the acrid smoke to the exit, is he going to say, 'So how's about grabbing some noodles later – that is, if this thing doesn't explode in a fireball?' Is he going to maintain his erection all the way down the escape slide? Perhaps in the event of a landing on water, when he's blowing on his whistle to attract Cheryl's attention, and Cheryl has managed to staunch the bleeding of the other surviving passengers clinging on to the debris, she'll swim over to him and, right before he succumbs to the ocean's icy embrace, Cheryl will finally give in to what has been undeniable ever since she saw him sit down in 3K, the most distinguished of all the aisle seats, and use her one remaining hand to jack him off.

Before long, National Airlines replaced the 'Fly me' ad, this time using one with a more Heraclitus-like tone: 'We'll fly you like you've never been flown before.' Aviation regulations would dictate otherwise. Commercial flight has never been a playground for mavericks, no matter how droll the in-flight announcements can get. What's going to happen is that they're going to fly you in the *exact same way as before*, with as few variations as possible. If your flight is from Luton to Corfu, there's one way it's going to pan out – i.e. you get on the plane, the plane takes off, the plane lands your broken ass in Corfu, you get off the plane, they pretend to clean the plane, then a bunch of other shit-kickers get on the plane, and the plane hauls *their* broken asses back to Luton, the jewel of Bedfordshire. If they're flying you in a way they haven't flown you before, that's because the engines have failed. And call me uptight, but the thought of falling to my death has seldom given me a boner.

Air Jamaica went with 'We make you feel good all over', which, even if you were just to focus on your inner ear, is a flat-out fib. Few things are guaranteed to make people feel worse than air travel. You are one hundred times more likely to catch a cold on a plane; you're exposed to more radiation than you would be if you stood next to a nuclear reactor; and perhaps most pressingly, it makes a man mighty windy. The moment right before flatus passes through the rectum is one of tension and intense self-hatred. Sure, once it's out you feel like God, but until your alimentary canal deflates, you want to die, and you don't care how.

Air France had the slogan 'Have you ever done it the French way?' But how can you fly in a way that's particularly 'French'? Does the plane wear a beret and leave a trail of Gauloises fumes? Are the in-flight announcements underscored by an accordion? Are other planes, especially if they're on their gap years, inexplicably attracted to them? What is so specifically *French* about these aircraft? Are they just giant winged baguettes? Or is the advertiser trying to suggest that the French cabin crew may well . . . well, what exactly? Why don't they just call it Caligulair? 'Our seats are wipe-clean for a reason . . .'

The 'Fly me' campaign was not the first time the promise of intimacy was used in airline marketing. In 1967, United made this inducement: 'Everyone gets warmth, friendliness and extra care – and someone may get a wife.' In fact, ever since Ellen Church (of whom more later) suggested that women work as stewardesses, the implication has been that these women are there *for* you . . .

Yet the effect of this marketing is to make the whole endeavour of being a stewardess seem trivial, unimportant and *unnecessary*. When something really is important, you don't rely on 'sex appeal'. If there were print ads for brain surgery, you wouldn't show a picture of a glamour model, next to the caption, 'Meet Cindy, she'll be holding the forceps . . .'

I Can't Believe Your Boyfriend Owns This Whole Houseboat

The title of this chapter is Christine's first line in the film, and it's a model of compression. Not only do we know that Donna, Christine and Sherry are on a houseboat (something that the wide shot showing them on a houseboat might have failed to convey), but we also discover that Sherry has a boyfriend. And what's more, he's the sole owner of a houseboat. Although we never meet Sherry's boyfriend, Herb, the fact that he owns a houseboat is enough to evoke an image of a man alive to the tax benefits of offshore living. No communal purchasing for Herb. That's his boat, from stern to prow.

Lots of chaps see fit to split a boat. Not Herb. None of this 'Would you mind getting the boat back to me for Thursday? I promised to take the old crate out with my father-in-law.' 'Get your own boat,' Herb would say, flashing that grin that makes it impossible to dislike him for too long. 'This one's mine.'

'I can't believe your boyfriend owns a percentage of this houseboat as part of a co-operative,' is a line that Christine might have uttered with a smidge less relish.

To impress Christine, you need to be the kind of guy

who can purchase a vessel outright.

Herb's unilaterally held houseboat is on Lake Havasu, which we know as the man-made reservoir behind Parker Dam on the Colorado river, between California and Arizona. And although the water is rich with delicious freshwater fish, particularly small- and largemouth bass, Donna, Christine and Sherry leave their rods and nets at home, electing instead to sunbathe.

But almost immediately the clasp on Donna's bikini breaks. This is one of the last things Donna expected to happen, and the malfunction is less than welcome. Sherry says that she thinks there may be some safety pins or something in a shoebox in the bedroom closet below deck. As far as Donna's concerned, Sherry thinking there may be some safety pins or something in a shoebox in the bedroom closet below deck is enough to persuade her to take a look. Wisely, Sherry doesn't say she's 100 per cent on the matter, but it's certainly worth a try. A safety pin or something from the bedroom closet would be just the ticket to effect a temporary repair. Is it a long-term solution? Of course it isn't. Sherry never pretended it was. She wants Donna to be comfortable. And how can Donna be comfortable when her wobblers are flapping in the cruel Arizona wind? Also, how can Sherry and Christine enjoy the sun under such circs? Clearly, measures need to be taken, and they need to be taken fast. So the best course is for Donna to re-tether her shame – no one wants to see her naked breasts – then, as soon as she's back on terra firma, head for the nearest swimwear shop and kit herself out with something that will steadfastly secrete her spheres from sight.

Exit Donna in search of said shoebox.

Enter, on a speedboat, shore patrolman Ted Stewart (Mark Ruffalo).

Ted tells Sherry that he's looking for Herb, who, for some unexplained reason, ran off with the former's flare gun. Chekhov's old dictum hits us with a Proustian gush: if you find a flare gun in the drawer in the first act, that flare gun is going to go off in the third. We file this information away in a mental drawer marked 'Set-Up'. But Barreto isn't about to task his audience with retaining information: this Chekhovian distress signal is moments away from a thrilling discharge.

Sherry tells Ted that he's welcome to check below deck to see if Herb is there, neglecting to mention that Donna has literally just gone below deck with her howlers unsheathed. One also wonders why Sherry doesn't know whether Herb is or is not on the houseboat. Particularly when the houseboat is in the middle of a lake. Is Herb the kind of boyf* who silently swims off a boat without

* Post-texting parlance for 'boyfriend'.

anyone knowing? Is Herb an assassin? Or is this just one of the many privileges of sole proprietorship? Sometimes Herb will be there, sometimes Herb won't be. You got a problem with that, take it up with the boat's owner: Herb.

Ted descends and finds no Herb, but soon locates the flare gun. Hearing suspicious sounds coming from one of the rooms, he kicks open the door, brandishing the recently retrieved flare gun, only to find a mortified Donna still struggling with her broken bikini top. Mercifully for both parties, she covers her trunk through a combination of quick thinking and careful hand placement, thus sparing us, the audience, from the unsettling prospect of seeing Gwyneth Paltrow partially nude. But her tender mercies are not so covered that our man could feel comfortable ploughing on with pleasantries. Ergo, Ted gallantly offers to fix the clasp by using the twist-tie prised from a plastic-wrapped loaf. Clearly, Ted Stewart is a man who cares more about human dignity than prolonging bread life, a fact not lost on Donna. It might be worth noting that the name 'Stewart' is of Old English origin and means 'guardian' or 'ward'. Will this Stewart come to steward the stewardess?*

Ted segues from embarrassment to cocksure couturier with admirable alacrity. When he returns with the

---

* Spoiler alert: yes.

twist-tie, he signals for Donna to turn around by whistling and making a circular gesture with his index finger. Not one minute earlier, the guy was gripping the butt of a signal pistol and pointing its barrel at our narrator. Now, our narrator is following *his* hand signal. It turns this 'meet cute' into a dance, a primal interplay of gesture and grooming. We no longer see Gwyneth Paltrow and Mark Ruffalo; we see two bonobo chimps duking it out for dominance, and it's thrilling.

Ted then suggests that he and Donna take a ride on his speedboat. He says that it's his official duty to give all newcomers a special guided tour on his boat. In less commanding hands than Ruffalo's this comment might seem predatory (we know it is unlikely that this is an official duty at all – it would be a logistical nightmare – and I doubt he's going to waste fuel ferrying around the ugly), but here it speaks of a spontaneous urge towards freedom, exploration and (yes) joy – things that we know are close to Donna's heart.

However, Christine Montgomery overhears the invitation and suggests that she tag along. It's an awkward moment, and the first indication that Christine might not straightforwardly occupy the role of ally. During the excursion (throughout which Christine is cloyingly forward despite Ted's evident disinterest – is there anything more obnoxious than a woman who instigates intimacy?),

Donna asks Ted how he became a shore patrolman. Ted reveals that he was on his way to becoming a big-shot attorney and that he had a hot law firm all lined up when he realised that there was more to life – that he wanted to eat, drink and enjoy himself. It's unclear why Ted is so convinced that pursuing a career in the law would countermand his basic nutritional needs, but he continues: 'I had this crazy idea that I would look for the thing that would make me most happy.' Again, we wonder why Ted views these desires as indicative of mental instability. Isn't the pursuit of happiness enshrined in the American Constitution? It seems that flare-gun-toting-ruggedly-handsome-easy-going-guys-with-twinkly-eyes-who-don't-suffer-from-motion-sickness are able to misuse language without repercussion. In cinema, there seem to be few things more attractive than a purportedly well-educated man who drops out to pursue muscle work (cf. *Road House* and the extensive analysis thereof in Gordy LaSure's *The Grip of Film**): a former management consultant restoring a tree house as a way to reconnect with his gifted nephew; an information security analyst on extended sabbatical, hand-painting the boat he's made

---

* It's actually *Richard Ayoade Presents:* The Grip of Film *by Gordy LaSure*. If they don't have it in your local bookshop, it's likely they've sold out. Impress on any staff member the imperative to not let the amount of stock drop below double figures, lest they embarrass themselves further.

from foraged lumber, his flecked chest dripping colour; an astrophysicist stripping an engine, the sinews on his arms smeared with blood and black gold. Dong follows ding. But back in reality, try quitting your highly remunerated white-collar position to go and work in a slaughterhouse because you like the feel of meat. Those near and dear may not be similarly charmed by your integrity, and will be quick to communicate their thoughts.

Ted asks Donna what she's doing next weekend.

Tantalisingly, the question remains unanswered. Barreto's restless editor will cut before we get the chance to know.

A View on Stewardship

'Then God said, "Let us make humankind in our image, according to our likeness; and let them have dominion over the fish of the sea, and over the birds of the air, and over the cattle, and over all the wild animals of the earth, and over every creeping thing that creeps upon the earth."' – Genesis 1:26

This passage from the Old Testament raises many questions: e.g. are there fish *not* of the sea? And if there are, do we get dominion over them too, i.e. is it our job to put them back in the water? And what about freshwater fish? Who's dealing with trout? Or do they come under the heading 'wild animals'? And if so, why doesn't God just say 'wild animals' at the beginning and tighten up the whole bit? Plus, who's handling cats? Like much in the Good Book, it's unclear how much of this thing is our fault and how much the Big Guy should shoulder.

This verse is also used to justify the idea that (Wo)Man has a duty of care to the earth and the creatures thereon/in/above. We are Stewards of the World. We should take care of it. But read the passage again. It doesn't talk of stewardship. It talks of *dominion*.

As far as I'm concerned, this here's *our* pool party: we can do whatever the flip we want. If we want to lay a log in the lagoon, *pas de prob*. (cf. my monograph: 'POO(LS) – A New Approach'). I have absolutely no qualms about the supposedly large quantities of fossil fuels used in aviation. What are we meant to do with all this oil? Leave it unburnt? That oil is for us! We should enjoy it! If God didn't want us to burn fossil fuel, He wouldn't have allowed a layer of mud to form over dead animals and plants at the bottom of the ocean and subjected them to heat and pressure over many millennia.

Stewardship is about taking care of something. You might steward an elderly relative into a rest home. You might steward or 'siphon' the capital released from selling an elderly relative's home (into, e.g., your secret family). But we should no more steward the earth than we should steward those weaker than us. They'll only drag *us* into the mud. And it will take an aeon before we can be successfully converted into lovely, easy-burning oil.

By contrast, cabin crew *should* steward. They *are* stewards. An air stewardess is a surrogate mother and, like our real mothers, should ensure our seat belts are on, over our blankets, and that we keep them visible when we're asleep. She should, like our mothers, offer us a selection of hot and cold snacks and be prepared to take card payments. Finally, when we leave, they, like

90

our mothers, should remove and, if necessary, destroy everything we've left behind.

There is a parable about stewardship that is worth careful consideration within this context. We find it in chapter 16 of Luke's gospel:

[1]Jesus told his disciples: 'There was a rich man whose manager was accused of wasting his possessions. [2]So he called him in and asked him, "What is this I hear about you? Give an account of your management, because you cannot be manager any longer."

[3]'The manager said to himself, "What shall I do now? My master is taking away my job. I'm not strong enough to dig, and I'm ashamed to beg – [4]I know what I'll do so that, when I lose my job here, people will welcome me into their houses."

[5]'So he called in each one of his master's debtors. He asked the first, "How much do you owe my master?"

[6]'"Nine hundred gallons of olive oil," he replied.

'The manager told him, "Take your bill, sit down quickly, and make it four hundred and fifty."

[7]'Then he asked the second, "And how much do you owe?"

'"A thousand bushels of wheat," he replied.

'He told him, "Take your bill and make it eight hundred."

[8]'The master commended the dishonest manager because he had acted shrewdly. For the people of this world are more shrewd in dealing with their own kind than are the people of the light. [9]I tell you, use worldly wealth to gain friends for yourselves, so that when it is gone, you will be welcomed into eternal dwellings.

[10]'Whoever can be trusted with very little can also be trusted with much, and whoever is dishonest with very little will also be dishonest with much. [11]So if you have not been trustworthy in handling worldly wealth, who will trust you with true riches? [12]And if you have not been trustworthy with someone else's property, who will give you property of your own?

[13]'No one can serve two masters. Either you will hate the one and love the other, or you will be devoted to the one and despise the other. You cannot serve both God and money.'

I related strongly to this piece of scripture. I, too, am not strong enough to dig and am easily tempted by discounts. But if you can't serve two masters, to which Coen brother should I address my comments? And how come there's 50 per cent off olive oil, but only 20 per cent off wheat? Also, why's this guy getting through so much olive oil? You should just lightly coat the bottom of the pan. It's also unclear whether 'eternal dwellings' refers to leasehold or freehold properties. But the passage *is* clear in encouraging us to buy friendships. We soon realise that no one truly rich (i.e. $10 million-plus in liquid assets) is without friends. The only way to have prevented Donald Trump's election would have been to bankrupt him, but he has too many bushels. That tangerine man's lousy with bushels.

Scriptural commentators suggest that this parable is an injunction to be as shrewd in spiritual matters as the 'worldly' are shrewd in material matters, but maybe those people should stay out of retail. If a man goes into Waitrose and they're out of bone broth, shit's gonna get real, real fast. When a man's screaming in the aisles, are they going to be spiritually shrewd or are they gonna restock?

By logical inference, Ryanair is certainly the most spiritual of airlines. With commendable consistency, they demonstrate their commitment to serving something other than mere people.

But will Ted Stewart be able to serve Donna's needs, or will he be the Ryanair of love interests?

Upgrading

Donna, Christine and Sherry sit at the counter of an airport diner. They are laughing at a joke or an anecdote, but we do not hear the set-up. This wonderful device, wherein the storyteller begins the scene during the chortle's apex, an ad-libbed line cresting over the froth ('And those kinds of stains don't come out' or 'I didn't know it could swell up like that!'), admirably adheres to the credo of every decent dramaturge: show up late and get out early.* Of course, we would love to know what these bubbly women were just talking about (the trick of fiction is to convince us that life spills out beyond the narrative's frame), but plot is all, and something's afoot . . .

The camera pans with a stewardess from another airline as she crosses behind our heroines and joins her two colleagues, Barreto's flair for dramatic mirroring in glorious evidence. These new, unfamiliar flight attendants are from a 'higher-class' airline, and they commence to boast about their lifestyles, while simultaneously speaking derogatively about Cleveland's cachet as a stop-over destination. They brazenly compare the various high-end

* Advice that our great nation took w/r/t EU membership.

94

products they have purchased on their international trips and then flounce off, while one of them 'comically' insists they might need to take a 'flea dip'.

As well as being incredibly mean-spirited, this is a bare-faced lie. This dame is *not* going to douse herself with insecticide at the next available opportunity. If she has anything like a regular hygiene routine and changes her clothes daily, she's *extremely* unlikely to get fleas. Fleas live off blood. They are rarely to be found in carpets and/or lounge seats. The comment is ignorant and specifically intended to wound! I love it when *Top* hits on truths like these! Some people are so up themselves!

Humiliated, Donna attempts to rally the team's spirits, insisting that they are every bit as good as 'they' (i.e. the demonstrably superior stewardesses) are. It's interesting that she should make this appeal on the basis of *equality*, when much of the narrative of *Top*, simply by locating Donna as both central protagonist and someone who can address the audience directly, leads us towards the unavoidable inference that Donna *is* better than everyone else. She's already the best flight attendant at Sierra Airlines, and we have every reason to believe her ascent will continue. Perhaps it would have been more honest for Donna to make an attestation of her superiority. But this is not the time to invoke a misreading of Nietzsche. Donna has had an idea (ably backed up by one of Barreto's masterfully informative insert shots). Royalty Airlines are holding a job fair this weekend at the Marriott hotel in San Francisco, and Donna thinks they should go!

We smash-cut to the trio driving along and singing to Bon Jovi's up-tempo ode to invocation, 'Livin' on a Prayer' (the original recorded version!). We don't even need voice-over to tell us that these young(ish) women have decided to attend the job fair! As the three of them fill in their application forms, Donna notices that Christine dots her 'i's with little hearts. The actresses play the scene so naturally that we might just feel it to be a charming character detail, but it's a carefully placed piece of information on which a crucial plot point will later turn. For now, the film races on towards a revealing interview montage conducted by Royalty Airlines' training supremo, John Witney (Mike Myers). Myers brings a marvellous energy and physicality to the role, playing Witney as cross-eyed, a medical condition from which much hilarity ensues. At the end of the gruelling process, only Christine and Donna survive, leaving the sadly underwritten Sherry to leave the film with no real end to her arc, though I like to think that she'll take the opportunity to commiserate, off screen, with Co-Pilot Steve.

The three stewardesses hug. Sherry tells Donna and Christine to study hard and make her proud. She then pats her flank and makes a hand gesture akin to a child pretending they're holding a gun. This gesture is copied in turn by Christine and Donna. The semiotics of this aren't immediately clear, and perhaps have their roots in a scene that was cut. In an interview about *Top*, Mark Ruffalo says that the film changed a lot and that there were reshoots. So, excitingly, there could be a deleted target-practice sequence languishing somewhere in the personal archives of one of *Top*'s three credited editors. In the same interview, Ruffalo says that he originally categorised the film as being like a seventies sex comedy, until they 'took most of the sex out of it'. It's unusual to hear an actor mention that a film ended up containing less sex (and presumably nudity?) than they'd originally hoped. Perhaps the gesture made by the three stewardesses has some tawdry backstory, now excised. But given that the 'thrust' of *Top* is the steely focus of Donna Jensen, determined to blast beyond her limited world of wind and lost balloons, when and with whom would the comedic coitus have occurred? That Jensen would have assignations with men other than Ted is unthinkable, especially post-Boulay. Could there have been satirical sex between Rob Lowe's character and one of the other stewardesses? Perhaps the nefarious Christine? It's possible, but it's hard to know what story function it would have had, and it would make his earlier encouragement of Donna take on a sinister undertone, as if his tips about turbulence were not meant sincerely. Lowe already looks like a man who's enjoying his own scent, so it's possible that he was simply trying to seduce, but to position the cabin as a place of sexual danger does not fit in with the quasi-bucolic Barretian universe.

Is it possible that Ruffalo's comment was disingenuous? He always looks to be mid-shrug, as if to imply, 'I can't believe I'm saying this either,' which can be an advantage for an actor, who, inevitably, will end up taking work of varying quality. Sometimes a heritage piece like *View from the Top* comes along, and all you have to do is hit your marks and let the script shine. But when faced with the plotless piddle of *You Can Count on Me* or the corrosive anti-family ideology of *The Kids Are Alright*, Ruffalo often looks like he's trying to shake off an invisible coat.

Perhaps he was merely revealing his own unconscious associations. As we discussed earlier, the air stewardess has long been a figure of male fantasy. The high altitude, restrictive headroom and limitless supply of tomato juice is intensely erotic and, for many men, a great opportunity to legitimately maintain eye contact with a woman who can only hide behind a curtain for so long.

The Flight Path of True Love
(Never Runs Smooth)

Donna's excitement at entering the enrolment programme is soon tempered when she goes on a date with Ted.

Interestingly, they choose to go to a restaurant. One of the excellent things about a film in which the main stars are seated so frequently is that you aren't distracted by a lot of scenery whizzing past in the background. You can just zero in on their faces and set about trying to work out what's whirring within. Ted kicks off proceedings by raising a toast* and congratulating Donna on her admittance to the Royalty Airlines training programme. Donna confesses to being nervous, that many people don't get past the first two weeks, and that she doesn't want to be among their number. Graciously, Ted contends that she will have no problems whatsoever: she is smart, beautiful

---

* One thing strikes the audience member immediately. Ted is raising a rather large glass of water, with which he chinks Donna's glass of red. Is Ted teetotal? Is he in recovery? Have there been troubled waters over which he's had to do a little bridge work? Also, Ted's drunk a good deal of the water in that massive glass. What kind of bladder does the man have? It's no good squirming while getting the download from Donna about her feelings/resentments/petty beefs about work colleagues, etc., as it might make him look less than scintillated.

and charming. Part of the job of Female Protagonist is to choose which Supporting Male to allow into your character's private thicket, and one way you can always tell whether a chap's the ticket is if he compliments you on your intelligence before your looks.

Here's a man who knows you've got the juice, but isn't going to bang on about what an absolute knockout you are before giving a tip of his hat to your glorious grey matter. Sure, you're a '10', a dime, a babe, but the first thing that struck our man, when he saw you in that tight dress as you walked towards him in slow motion while the camera tilted up from your high heels fully taking in any movement that happened to occur twixt hips and hair flick, was that tremendous brain of yours. 'There', he said to himself, 'is a bonce for the ages. This woman's an all-round intellect. I can't fault her spatial perception, and she seems strong linguistically, kinaesthetically and administratively.' No wonder the Supporting Male looks so flustered. He hasn't seen someone so mentally on top of things since he can't remember when, and it's only at that point that he stops and thinks, 'Hang on, the surface elements aren't too shabby either.' Ted plays a straight bat, keeps his wits, and lobs in another generic compliment ('charming') so it doesn't look like he's some kind of demented sociopath bifurcating all and sundry into brains and brawn.

This is not to dismiss the importance of looks. It's very important to be good-looking, if only because the alternative is to be bad-looking. You can't really expect any half-decent dude to 'have', let alone 'hold', a dog's dinner. That's just the law of the jungle. If your face is neither fish nor fowl, but rather a mixture of the two, then the male gaze may not alight. Best to stay behind closed doors and secure the Chubb lock.

Take Mike Myers's John Witney. One of his eyes points the wrong way. It's funny, fiendishly so, but is it romantic? Clearly not. The idea of Mike Myers's John Witney finding love is farcical. He could no more be a Romantic Lead than a tube of pâté or a turd.* There's often something, well, sneaky about ugly people. Some have a squint, or one leg shorter than the other, or a stoop, or a thatched neck, or teeth that don't seem to be playing on the same team, and the whole effect is one of making you wonder where you are with them. Whereas when faced with something smooth, symmetrical and clean, one gets a distinct whiff of the divine, a celestial scent that lets you know God's done His work and all is well.

Donna knows an orator when she sees one and she says as much, commending Ted on one hell of a pep

---

* *Shallow Hal*, another standout Paltrow vehicle, addresses this with eloquence.

talk, even though it was more of a pep sentence. But the woman looks as sparkling as a freshly scrubbed pan, and we're ready to forgive any vagaries. How much harder it is to take such imprecision from the foul of face. It makes you realise the true value of movie stars! At the time of going to print, Robert Downey Jr has earned $50 million and climbing for *Iron Man 3*. You may think this outrageous, but just take a look in the mirror. Do you want a permanent record of the disappointment? Do you want to exhibit footage of your rancid reflection?* We see here a simple principle of the market: when 'demand' = the entire planet and 'supply' = one (Downey Jr), you can dictate your own cheques.

Ted bats away the compliment, sweeping away any praise for his eloquence into the path of his parents, whom he describes as 'big cheerleaders'. Ted has a wonderfully suggestive way of painting pictures with words, doesn't he? 'No point saying how great I am, Donna, it's all nurture. Cossetted and cooed, cheeks pink from pinching, puffed up with hot air, smothered in soothing oil, here lies a stranger to opprobrium.' But Ted's attestation robs him of agency. 'My ability to give on-the-spot exhortation is not down to my native gifts,' he implies, with an angled tilt of the head, his mouth chewing a restrained

* For additional complexity, try talking fast while smirking . . .

bite of movie food. 'It was given to me. Imparted, if you will, by my parents.'

But Donna's Mom was an ex-showgirl. Her uncredited dad went to children's parties exclusively to drink beer. What chance did Donna have? No off-the-cuff speeches for her. She lacks the breeding. When you start to unpack the statement, it starts to feel incredibly insulting. What looks like modesty is actually a quasi-fascist argument either for genetic supremacy or the absolute necessity of being correctly encoded within a family unit. It's a far-right conservative's charter: one infant bathed in balm, the other forced to endure the incessant gustiness of Nevada, unable to light so much as a birthday candle without it fatally guttering. In such circs, a girl doesn't even have the strength to hold on to her balloon. 'Let it fly,' she thinks. 'I don't know how much longer I can stand the strain.'

Donna, squashing down her envy, quotes Sally as saying that the greatest asset you can have is someone who believes in you. Two things strike the viewer. Firstly, (s)he wonders whether there is a danger in turning human relationships into 'assets'. Secondly, (s)he asks herself why is Donna talking as if Ted will know who the hell Sally is? Ted, reading our minds, asks if Sally is 'like her aunt or something'. Donna says that Sally's more of a friend.

This is one of the few exchanges in the film where we wonder whether Donna is one pickle short of a ploughman's. Is she constructing an elaborate fantasy in which Sally Weston, a woman whom she's never met, is *already* her friend?

Let's recap the scene:

Curtain up.

1. Donna nervous about flight attendant training.
2. Ted convinced she'll be great.
3. Donna impressed by Ted's exhortation.
4. Ted cites the importance of parental support.
5. Donna quotes Sally Weston's wisdom.

Finis.

As they exit LuLu's (French cuisine?), it's almost clear from Donna's facial expressions that she's enjoyed her time with Ted. She casually mentions that she's having a goodbye party. Ted declines the offer, saying that he would be unable to hide his disappointment that she is leaving so soon. It sounds sweet, but there's an ominous undercurrent. Unable to celebrate the success of others, Ted knows that he would spend the evening brooding in the corner, stewing at each interaction which did not involve him, furious that his will had been thwarted.

Inexplicably aroused by his petulance, Donna begins to lean in to him, a glazed expression in her eyes.

Ted pivots to be at even more of an angle. Ruffalo, an ex-high-school wrestler, often looks to be readying himself to receive a blow. But when their faces are little less than twelve inches apart, Ted stops himself. Is it Donna's wine-soaked breath? An old wrestling injury? His stated reason is that the 'only kiss we've got here is a goodbye kiss, which, as kisses go, are not my favourite'. But couldn't he have worked this out when he was at a decent distance from the woman? And why is he creating this bizarre taxonomy of kisses? One fears Ted notes each oral interaction in his little snog log and grades them for firmness, moistness and ferocity. 'Dear Snog Log. Today was a bad day. I was hoping for some I'm Staying in Cleveland Tongue, but I had to keep it in the cave.'

Donna's training programme is in Texas, so that's where Donna's going to go. If you want to reach the Top and thence View, you go to Texas and you train like hell and you shut up about what kind of kisses you like. Perhaps Donna needed some physical release before she knuckled down. Maybe she wanted the oblivion of consequence-free congress. Or is Ted unable to give her even that?

Earlier we talked about the Parable of the Unjust Steward. Has Ted Stewart been unjust here? Should he have aped Tommy Boulay and given Donna the gift of his girth? At the end of the parable, Jesus warns, 'No man can serve two masters,' and if we were to imagine that he was talking about women as well as men, this could well apply to Donna Jensen. Can she serve her ambition and romance?

Another well-placed VO allows her to deepen the dilemma of Free Will: 'Why can't all choices be simple? Window or aisle? Coffee or tea? Not career or romance . . .' In short, why can't life be idiomatically similar to air travel? Yet for me, 'window' or 'aisle' isn't a simple choice, and if I haven't checked in online, it's often not a choice at all. I like to look out of the window so I can be the first to see if a wing goes missing, but I also have a weak bladder and dislike hurdling over the prone.

Is it too fanciful to think that if people had travelled by plane during the life of Christ, he might have used the language of aviation during his teachings? Perhaps he would have ended the Parable of the Unjust Steward by saying, 'No plane can have two pilots.'

¹But a Pharisee, who wanted to trap Jesus, said, 'What about the co-pilot?'
²And Jesus said unto him, 'The captain is the legal commander. The co-pilot only takes over if the captain has been incapacitated. That's basic.'

[3]And another Pharisee, who was wise in the way of aviation law, though his heart was hard, replied, 'But doesn't the co-pilot or "first officer" normally share control with the pilot, designating one as the "PF" or "pilot flying", while the other is termed the "PNF" or "pilot not flying"?

[4]And Jesus, knowing they wished to trap him, said, 'It doesn't matter who's flying the plane, the buck stops with the captain. He alone is responsible for the aircraft, its passengers and its crew.'

[5]'Except in the case of incapacitation,' said a Pharisee.

[6]'An incapacitated pilot is no longer able to pilot, so we're getting into ontology here,' said Jesus.

[7]'But you will agree that there are two pilots,' said another Pharisee.

[8]'There's a pilot and co-pilot. That's different to two pilots and it's different to two co-pilots. Just as Ant and Ant is not the same as Dec and Dec, nor is Dec without Ant Ant 'n' Dec, but something other, and not the One True Union, no matter how good Holly Willoughby might be,' said Jesus.

[9]When the chief priests heard this, they were amazed, and not only because they wondered how long before the reference would date. [10]And they phoned their Uncle Levi and told him what Jesus had

said, which took quite a while, because he said he didn't know who Holly Willoughby was, and they didn't believe him.

As he and Donna part, the camera tracks into Ted, trapped in his puritanical bubble, while Donna paces off, no doubt to frig herself unconscious. The soundtrack swells to the sound of 'Time After Time', the song made famous by Cyndi Lauper. The cover by Katie Cook is so faithful that it's only on the level of your subconscious that you realise something's missing. This dissatisfaction cleverly mimics the thoughts that we might read into Ted's face, if we weren't so angry with him.

The 'undercarriage' of the scene, though, refers back to the Parable of the Unjust Steward. Can one serve one's 'work/career' *and* 'family/relationships'? We will discuss this at much greater depth in the dueness of course.

For now, it's a conflict so big that it needs its own musical motif.

'Time After Time'

For most of us, the title 'Time After Time' will evoke the 1979 film in which the author H. G. Wells (Malcolm McDowell) travels into the future to capture mass murderer Jack the Ripper (David Warner), who, to his sobering litany of barbarism, has now added 'time machine theft'. But for others, the title is that of a song, the title of which was taken from the film.

'Time After Time', written by Cyndi Lauper and middle-school survivor Rob Hyman, was the second single from Lauper's debut album *She's So Unusual*, which has sold 16 million copies worldwide, proving that it's possible to feel unusual en masse. A last-minute addition to the LP, 'Time After Time' went on to become Lauper's first US number one, and in the year 2000, *Rolling Stone* magazine ranked it as the sixty-sixth best pop song of all time (although how much credence one can give a list that only places the Backstreet Boys' 'I Want It That Way' at number ten I don't know).

Certainly, while listening to 'Time After Time', the fact that you could be enjoying one of sixty-five statistically superior pop songs barely troubles you. You are rolled up in a carpet of melody and hoisted onto a shoulder of empowerment bettered only by the Spice Girls' under-appreciated 'Spice Invaders', the implied subtitle for the film *Dune*.

In the video for 'Time After Time', director Edd 'Two Ds' Griles shows us a static caravan, isolated in a wood.* Within, Lauper watches the 1936 tearjerker *The Garden of Allah*, in which Charles Boyer competes for Marlene Dietrich's attention with a series of ornamental vases. Lauper mouths along to the dialogue, so we know that either she's a synth-pop savant or she's seen the film multiple times. Her lover sleeps beside her. In movies, and perhaps in life, nothing seems to anger a woman more than a man who can share her bed and sleep at the same time. 'Look at him,' she seems to say, 'lowering his core body temperature, repairing cells, consolidating memory, his slack mouth failing to form any words of appreciation, his pallid back a scarcely scalable obstacle to pastures new.'

Lauper is out of the trailer before she can give her giant porcelain dog a farewell stroke. Her lover, woken out of his disgraceful slumber by the slam of the Winnebago door, dashes out to find he still has time to catch her during her slow walk towards the camera, but it's to no avail: she's already dissolving into flashback. Lauper bitterly recalls a moment in a diner when he failed to actively

* Prefiguring *Top*'s first post-title frame.

support her new hairstyle. The moment was public, and therefore fatal. When Cyndi Lauper shows you her new hairstyle for peer approval, all you can do is applaud and hope the resultant retinal damage isn't long-lasting. Her hair is the colour of a radioactive energy drink. Lauper sees no way for relations to continue, though she graciously allows her lover to drive her to the train station. On the platform, she reassures her drowsy paramour that she will always wait for him, right before disappearing in a puff of steam.

As the camera cranes up, her lover bows his head in repentance (one hopes) for his inability to know a good haircut when he sees one, but one fears that he's nodded off again.

As she sits on the train, moving on to better things, while a single glycerine tear fights its way through foundation so thick it might need its own foundation, the parallels with *Top* are uncanny.

The version of 'Time After Time' in *View from the Top* is by Katie Cook, and with all due deference to whoever Ms Cook is, her version can't match the original. Even Cyndi Lauper couldn't match the original: it has since become her signature tune, as sure as my signature scent is spicy. Lauper had the ability to make every yelp sound like a sob, and every sob like a cry of defiance. Without 'Time After Time', how else would a tired teen drama conclude its eighties-themed prom finale? It would have to use '(I've Had) The Time of My Life' or Billy Joel's 'The Longest Time'.

Time and romance are inextricably linked because as soon as anything starts, it starts to end. Apart from, it often seems, *View from the Top. View from the Top* feels unending. It's like a dream from which you wake, only to realise you were dreaming that you were dreaming. Which is why the choice of 'Time After Time' is so perfect. It gently speaks, and often squawks, of the cyclical nature of all narrative. When you hear the song, you feel you've heard it before, and you have. Because the story's an old one: a lover leaves, leaving nothing behind but generalities.

Lauper promises to catch her lover if he falls, while continually walking away from him. What if, while watching one of her Grammy acceptance speeches, her lover falls over from some unrelated boredom? Is she going to leap from the podium and cradle him before he keels back into Beyoncé? Whenever I fall, it's rare to find a catcher in the receiving position. Purported 'loved ones' won't stop laughing until I prove to them that the puddling blood is mine, and even then it's not a given. When I see someone fall, the only thing I catch is my breath, before leaving the vicinity, lest I feel compelled to use up my valuable time pretending to help.

Lauper promises her lover that if he's lost, he can find her, if only he'll look. And from the way she looks, like she's wearing everything she's ever owned and will own in the future, it seems like she'd stand out in a crowd. But Lauper's so short that the crowd would all have to stand out of the way. Mere looking might not be enough. Given how reluctant he is to leave his trailer, and how fond of travel she seems to be, he might need to employ a dragnet. Is Lauper really authorising a manhunt?

All this speaks of the conflict between heart and head. Lauper's head is trying to work out the logistics of remaining accessible while leaving for ever, but her heart can't forgive her lover for how well rested he seems to be. In the conflict between heart and head, Donna is resolved: head wins. But reject the heart, and it may turn and bite you in the ass, no matter how much of a hard-ass you pretend to be . . .

PART FOUR:
THE LIFE OF SKY

A View Under Weston's Wing

Donna can't believe it.

Sally Weston is going to be her personal mentor.

Sally. Weston.

And what's more, Sally Weston is inviting a select group of candidates to her really big house.

And further to *that*, we then cut to an exterior shot of this really big house.

And in case we're *still* unsure of how really big this house is after the shot of the candidates entering its really big hall, one of the candidates says, 'This is a really big house.'

The *mise en scène* is impeccable. Barreto's camera joins Weston as she stands at the top of a double staircase. She looks down on our would-be flight attendants, her view (literally) *from the top*, while the song 'Up, Up and Away' by the 5th Dimension subtextually thwacks any nails not yet hit squarely on their heads by the audible gasps.

In the following dining-room scene, which operates as an exponential multiplier of both exposition and eyelines, we are able to hear about how Sally reached her vaulted position. She met her handsome husband, Jack Weston (Chad Everett), in first class. He asked for a surfeit of warm nuts, and she realised that what he wanted wasn't safe to put in a microwave. His face blending seamlessly with his fitted leather jacket, Jack looks like he'd rather be wrestling a steer than interact with Randy Jones (Joshua Malina), the crew's comic relief. When Randy asks to be treated as just one of the girls, Jack's eyes visibly dim. It's a fun moment and taps into the truth of how uncomfortable it is to be suddenly confronted, in one's own home, with an insistent homosexual. What must make it even more galling is that Jack built this home himself, using hands that are as adept at felling a log as cupping the breast of a new secretary; hands that have touched no penis other than his own, and only then to uncork a jet of steaming piss or to purposively guide his gift into a Playmate of the Year's glistening cove.

It's a shame we don't get to see more of Jack and his barely contained disgust. This scene is his swansong. What we see more of, though, is the connection between (Sally) Weston and Jensen. Even though Weston and Jensen sounds like the diffusion line of a gun range, these two are a class act, linked by their glossy manes, nostalgia for the lost magic of air travel, a mania for handing out tiny meals at altitude, and Barreto's matching slow zooms.

In a way that could be creepy in less assured hands than Candice Bergen's, Sally surprises Donna as the latter walks out of the former's animal-print-lined bathroom. Donna has just been admiring a collection of red and green aeroplane-shaped soaps and is understandably overwhelmed. Sally takes Donna to look at her walk-in wardrobe. Donna can't believe that one person could own all of these clothes. My thoughts turn, as I'm sure do yours, to moth management. Sometimes people ask me what I do, and the correct answer is 'almost nothing', but if pressed, I might say that I'm a writer. But that is a lie. What I really do is battle moth. How anybody can simultaneously believe in a loving God and moth is beyond my comprehension.

The savagery of moth is chilling. The only way to beat the bastards is to encase everything you own in plastic and suck out all the air; you have to live like a budget astronaut. But the alternative is that the bastards win. Do you realise that moth mouths are so deformed they don't eat? They take in all the nourishment they need for their ghastly lives while they're in the larval stage. What kind of animal doesn't snack?

Moth don't snack.

What kind of monster eats cravats?

Moth eat cravats.

Sally tells Donna she senses a hunger in her, and indeed, both women look hungry. Neither one looks like a complex carbohydrate has passed their lips since the mid-nineties. Sally says she once had the same hunger. Hunger for Paris, First-Class International.

Sally then makes Donna say 'Paris, First-Class International' over and over again. Donna closes her eyes, and the image melts into some iconic stock footage of the City of Lights. The effect is powerful, an auto-suggestive incantation that feels almost ritualistic. Is Barreto echoing *Rosemary's Baby*, or is the synchronicity accidental?

Before we have the chance to realise the question doesn't matter, the movie snaps out of this reverie and into a dizzying sequence in which Mike Myers's John Witney puts the trainees through their paces. It's a breathless display of (presumably improvised) zaniness – as if Barreto said, 'Mike, we've booked you for three days – all of your scene-work is either behind a desk or in one or two other indoor locations – we have the script – that's our bible – but once we get what's on the page, feel free to fly.'

Some of Witney's claims (e.g. that he's felt a polar bear's nuts) are completely outlandish, but such fun! The underlying story is so strong, we are free to enjoy the anarchic comedic energy of what already feels like a canonical training montage. The only thing we miss is a reportedly excised set piece about how to handle terrorists, which the filmmakers thought might not play well in a post-Twin Towers world. It's a shame that it was not included on the DVD as a deleted scene, so that we could judge for ourselves: it could have helped us all heal. It is probably too much to say that the worst excesses of the Bush regime could have been avoided, but we'll never know what might have been.

While Donna takes her work very seriously and (unsurprisingly) excels, Christine struggles. We know that Donna is working hard because she is always taking notes and listens to John Witney's audio CD *That's Procedure* on her personal headphones. We know Christine isn't working hard because she is always yawning. And it is while giving a pep talk to the sleepy stewardess* that Donna notices something: Christine has taken some of the plane-shaped soaps from the bathroom in Sally Weston's house. Respectfully, but with a tone that conveys the gravity of the situation, Donna confronts Christine, who in turn insists that the soaps are clearly intended to be gifts for guests. Donna lets the matter drop, but another seed of doubt is planted in her private soil.

On my first watch of *View from the Top* (how I envy me then, as the film unspooled for the first time!) I was 120 per cent behind Donna, even though that's mathematically impossible. Christine's claim seems absurd.

* Influenced by Ted?

The soaps weren't wrapped! How could you transport them without compromising their integrity? But on subsequent watches (I've watched at least part of the film every day for three years) my position has softened.

Let's review.

Christine is face down on her bed, crying about how she has no particular talents. Donna, with whom she shares quarters, walks over to the dresser to retrieve a tissue. While there, she looks down at an open drawer and sees an unzipped sponge bag containing perhaps three or four plane-shaped soaps. Freud might say this was intentional on Christine's part: she *wanted* to be found out, but let's not get mired down in an explication of Christine's unconscious desires. When Donna asks where Christine got the soaps, Christine immediately says they're from Sally Weston's house. Now, why would she be so ready to admit whence she got them if she thought she was doing something underhand? Donna then makes a judgement: she accuses Christine of stealing. Christine says that these soaps are for guests. Donna counters by saying that they're for guests to *use*, not *take*. However, if the soaps are only for *use*, why would there be so *many* soaps in the dish? There are *eight* soaps in the (oddly deep) soap dish. Even after heavy soiling, you'd be hard pressed to get through two miniature aeroplane soaps. Also, after using one, are you meant to put it back in the

122

dish containing seven other soaps? Unless you were to dry that soap, the bottom of that dish is going to water-log and the other soaps are going to become mush.

Also, an aeroplane is a very frustrating shape for a soap to be. Sooner or later, the wings are going to snap off, leaving you with only the fuselage. Do you discard the wings? That makes it look like you're lathering up with a deathtrap.

If Sally Weston had any humanity, she would have only one soap on the go at any given time, refreshing the dish regularly. Also, and this needs to be said, why are these soaps so small? If you make *anything* small, you're implicitly saying, 'Here, take it.' If you see a bowl of mini-chocolates, I defy you not to scoop up at least three. This also applies to small fruit (e.g. grapes – 'Please take one'), but not large fruit (e.g. a pineapple – 'Keep your stinking hands to yourself'). Difficulty arises with medium-sized fruit. You are entitled to take an apple, but it is best to ask permission. A small satsuma, take and keep schtum. A mango, even if small, leave.

So where does this leave us?

1. Weston put out these soaps to deliberately entrap.
2. Weston has stolen these soaps from her time as a stewardess, stockpiled them, and is now trying to palm them off as her own.

3. Weston commissioned these soaps herself.
4. Weston bought the soaps.

If '1' is true, she's evil. If '3' is true, she's deranged. Who commissions their own soap *solely* for their own domestic use? If you are commissioning soap like that, you can't just get a few bars a year – the factory would laugh in your face; you would have to order hundreds – which points to their being, essentially, promotional items.

Unless Weston's hand-moulding these soaps herself, in which case – and I don't mean to demean anyone's mental state – she's having a breakdown.

W/r/t '4', who the hell sells aeroplane soaps? No one. I've searched extensively online so that I could complete my Sally Weston tribute room, and there's nothing. The only available aeroplane soap has received a very negative one-star review on Amazon: 'It came broken and over-priced for how tiny it was. DO NOT ORDER!!' As I feared, there's something inherently problematic with the structure of this genre of soap.

So, best guess is '2'. Just before she left the profession, Weston filled up her carry case.

We've all walked through the corridor of a travel tavern, seen one of those trollies filled with tiny soaps, shampoos and pens-that-work-for-no-longer-than-an-hour, checked for visible staff members, trousered as much as possible and sprinted for the lifts. That's not theft, that's sporting spirit. I now have enough tiny bottles of conditioner to last me till Valhalla.

Dear Lord, why would anyone, let alone Sally Weston, begrudge anyone taking seven or eight bars of novelty aeroplane soap?

The 'Golden Age':
A View in Hindsight

On 12 February 1930, a nurse and trained pilot called Ellen Church visited Steven Stimpson, one of the managers at Boeing, with a proposal.

Perhaps women could be of use during cabin service.

The idea was audacious. Women . . . looking after people . . . and being paid for it! How would they fit their hips through the aisles? If the plane was in trouble, would the pilot really have time to come out of the cockpit to staunch their tears? But Church, wisely, suggested that these women would be no ordinary useless women, they would be trained nurses: superwomen hardened at the sharp end of a scalpel. The whole thing sounded dubious, but Stimpson saw a way of packaging the deal. It was a different path to his previous idea of exclusively using young Filipino males, but maybe it could work. Like all true men of action, he immediately wrote a memo:

It strikes me that there would be great psychological punch to have young women stewardesses . . .
Imagine the national publicity we could get from

it, and the tremendous effect it would have on the traveling public.

What strikes me is, when did Ellen Church say anything about these stewardesses being young?

ELLEN: Sure they can nurse, Stimpsy – they can nurse like gangbusters – but the thing I want to stress is how *immature* some of these dames are. They're barely out of their teens . . .
STEVIE: Keep talkin' . . .
ELLEN: You know how when you're in danger, the only person who can reassure you is a really *young* female . . .
STEVIE: Keep talkin' . . .
ELLEN: Say you've just lost an arm – you're super-bummed about it – but you look up, and a nineteen-year-old is applying your tourniquet. You're passing out from the pain, but look how smooth her skin is!
STEVIE: Is she pretty, Ellen?
ELLEN: She is, Stimps. She's real pretty. You don't even know how pretty she is.
STEVIE: I never liked that stupid arm anyway.

Stimpson managed to persuade Boeing's board to go with the idea, but only if the nurses weren't so young that their tits hadn't had a chance to grow. Within a few years, the need for nursing qualifications was dropped – youth, tailored uniforms and attractiveness being deemed more than sufficient replacements for the ability to save lives. The airlines were faced with a catch-22: they sought to comfort those frightened of flying by providing cabin crew to help with safety, but they had to make it clear that the cabin crew weren't really needed for safety because the planes were already so massively safe.

Thus, the stewardesses came to be presented as merely decorative. They were receptionists without the administrative burden, maids without the elbow room. If women weren't afraid to be on a plane, why should anyone else be? Plus, if a woman were forced to share the same contained space as you, an emotionally closed-off businessman, how would she stop herself falling in love? Has she any idea how many moves you have? Has she any idea how many women would fall prey to your charms if only they were employed to pretend to like you? Flying was like a cocktail party where the guests were so magnanimous that they invited the staff to sit with them a little while.

After the end of World War II, with much of the female workforce displaced by returning soldiers, women found their employment options limited. The application rate for stewardesses was huge. Several thousand applicants would compete for a score of jobs, and the airlines rightly filtered out the unsightly. Becoming a stewardess allowed women to take on a role that was uniquely feminine: A Blank Canvas Onto Which Men Could Project Their Desire. But these women weren't just sexually objectified, they were also forced to conform to a male idea of female elegance. Stewardesses had to dress the same, have their hair cut the same way and walk as if they were miming being a teapot.

It is to these times that Sally Weston wishes to return.

Here is a woman who pines for a time when people dressed up for air travel, instead of wearing flip-flops and a T-shirt saying, 'I'm allergic to mornings.'

A time when stewardesses were grounded at the age of thirty-two for being past their best, both in terms of looks and temperament. (By then, their faces would begin to sag, and businessmen would not be able to fantasise about having intercourse with them without reflecting wistfully on the tragic cruelty of a beauty that fades.)

Weston yearns for a time when there wasn't a single non-Caucasian stewardess in the whole of North America. A time when Aloha Airlines' flight attendants were required to hula-hoop and play the ukulele.

A time when a stewardess could weigh no more than 115 lbs lest she destabilise the plane.

A time when an applicant for the job of stewardess would be asked to let the airline know if she had disproportionately large feet, so that they save both parties the disappointment of an interview.

A time when a stewardess could not be married for fear that the guilt caused by her absence from her husband's side would render her unable to concentrate.

A time when you could not be a stewardess and have visible scars, even though all scars, by definition, are visible.

A time when, owing to the rules about being single, non-pregnant and in your twenties, there was no prospect of increased pay or advancement, the job being a prelude to the domesticity for which it was a de facto training ground.

An elegant time.

A better time.

There is, still, an unpleasant elephant in the walk-in wardrobe, and that is the question of where all this *leads . . .*

Sally Weston tells Donna to never let go of her dream. However, the Sally Weston Plan only works if your dream is to be an air stewardess and never ask the question, 'And then what?' If your dream is to see Paris, but only in very short bursts, or to hear the word 'playfulness' used to justify sexual harassment, then those dreams can absolutely work under the umbrella of the primary Becoming-an-Air-Stewardess dream, but that's about it.

The implication seems to be that, by dint of her focus in the aisles, Sally Weston has acquired all of this wealth. But her wages alone could not buy a 'really big house'. And although Sally's book seems like an absolute banger, it's only just been published. Those royalties take a while to trickle through, believe me.

Like Sally, Donna's main chance of wealth is to meet and marry a wealthy person. Thus, the stewardess is a debutante, a debutante who has to do her own catering and clean up after the guests depart.

How will Donna meet this wealthy person? There is always the chance that someone flying in first class might not be despicable. There's a chance that such a person isn't horrendous and spoilt. There might be a genuine, mutual attraction. And there's a chance that that attraction might be free from the dangerous corrosion of the attendant power imbalance. It's very possible that a good relationship can spring up between a wealthy older man and a younger woman who has to bring him refreshments whenever he presses a button. That's what happened with Sally Weston and the leathery, homophobic, grunting love of her life.

But even if this *were* possible, Donna has already met Ted! Donna's not going to get rich like Sally Weston did, because Donna's not going marry a man who is *already* rich. Perhaps Ted can *become* rich, but that's not going to happen any time soon. And in the meantime, no one ever got rich handing out complimentary ramekins of hot nuts.

In her seminal survey of the stewardess, *Femininity in Flight: A History of Flight Attendants*, author Kathleen M. Barry brings her story to a close in the seventies, confining the post-seventies era to the briefest of epilogues, the implication being that by the time Jimmy Carter signed the 1978 Airline Deregulation Act, the Golden Age of air travel was over. Certainly, this is Sally Weston's view, so why is she recommending that Donna enter a profession so clearly in decline?

An Obstructed View

An exam hall. Barreto's camera tracks past a distressed, flustered Christine towards a smiling, confident Donna. A less thorough director might have left it at that, forcing the viewer to divine the hearts of these two individuals from mere surface signs. But Barreto, the man who brought us *One Tough Cop*, starring Stephen Baldwin as an Italian American police officer who alternates between smiling like someone who's apologised for farting but still finds it funny, and pouting so hard it looks like crime arouses him, is not going to rely on the accidental facial arrangements of actors. Thus, a colleague turns to Donna and asks how she's feeling w/r/t the test/results thereof. Big D's answer is emphatic: 'New York, here I come.'

So we need not imagine Donna's surprise when the published results indicate that she is very much not going to New York, and that Christine has 'landed' the coveted route. Paltrow's expression gives us a decent clue that things might not be as she'd hoped, but when we find her in John Witney's office insisting that there must be some kind of mistake, the full extent of the injustice is made manifest. Donna feels jibbed and cannot accept the results as they stand. She was number one in her class! Witney was there! Can't he see that (with due respect to his condition)?!

A stickler for 'procedure', Witney denies Donna's request to resit the test. He's seen this kind of thing before. Donna peaked too soon. But she refuses to back down. She can't go back to commuter service. How dare Witney stand in the way of her destiny?

It appears that the word 'destiny' is something of a trigger for Witney. He explodes with rage, poignantly revealing that he had wanted to be a flight attendant himself, but that he couldn't because of his cross-eyes. He is particularly dismissive of the value of eye exams. Winston Churchill said, 'Success is the ability to go from failure to failure without losing your enthusiasm.' But he never said anything about letting go of your fury. Fury is something you *need*, and if someone tells you otherwise, try screaming at them. They'll often go quiet and start to cry. That's when you know you've won.

Chastened, Donna accepts her fate. She is posted to the distinctly unglamorous Royalty Express – a budget division of the airline based in Cleveland. Donna is downcast: the hair is flat, announcements are drawled and she's sporting a smoky eye. But Donna Jensen isn't going to let failure stop her ascent. For a start, her new flight partner is the homosexual man, Randy Jones, who will serve as a reviving tonic after the toxic femininity of her undermining cohort, Christine.

Donna also reminds herself of her trajectory, putting up two posters on her thin leasehold walls: one of the Eiffel Tower, and the other of the equally evocative Arc de Triomphe. Together, they form a poignant visual representation of her goals, while the diegetic soundtrack of French-language cassettes provides audio accompaniment. She takes off the heavy eye make-up and adopts a fresher, brighter, 'can-do' skin tone.

Donna is Churchill's daughter after all.

In Which We Briefly Re-Route for Some Thoughts Concerning (a) Hair Height and (b) the Film *Sliding Doors*. We Hope You Aren't Overly Inconvenienced by the Delay

HAIR HEIGHT

There's an unspoken rule w/r/t this in post-Reagan America: high hair = low class.*

As *View from the Top* progresses, Donna's hair gets less high, her make-up more 'subtle', her clothes less clingy. Like a reverse Samson, her power grows as her follicles flatten. She moves from being 'other' to 'us', if we looked like Gwyneth Paltrow.

Thus, the 'make-over' scene in any Hollywood film is not really about *changing* how someone looks, it's about *restoring* someone's looks. It's about taking something aberrant and normalising it. Thus, femininity is an aesthetic democracy: we, the people, want women to be sunny yet demure, alluring yet chaste.

---

* Although the beehive is a category apart: both mobster wife and bohemian aristo.

For men, the opposite applies. The higher the hair, the greater the power. Sean Penn, Kurt Russell, Robert Redford: they're all thatch. And the thicker the thatch, the hotter the temper. If your hair's as high as Pacino's, you can go from low simmer to shrieking puce in less than a second, the head no more than the dot below an exploding exclamation mark. The height of your hair illustrates the emotional bandwidth in which you may operate, which is why Chris Walken can emphasise the syllable which *he* deems appropriate rather than the one that might convey meaning.

My hair is sometimes high, but it is also wide, and post-Einstein/Doc from *Back to the Future*, any *intelligence* associated with hair width is offset by an assumed craziness: you're the kind of customer who's too dazed to wipe the soot from your safety goggles after a comical chemical explosion. 'We're close! I just need to recalibrate the metrics,' you say, before collapsing onto an off-camera crash mat.

But there can also be power in having *zero* hair height, i.e. total baldness. A man who shaves his own head displays a vehement opposition to imperfection. 'Unless my hair provides complete coverage,' such a man says, 'I will destroy it.' This started with Brynner (Yul), continued with Willis, and reached its logical conclusion in Statham. These are some of the classiest thespians ever to avenge the inhumanity of Man by taking the law into their own chunky hands.

And as the hair gets lower, so does the voice. If your hair's low, talk slow. Otherwise, you're just a shrieking baldy. Audibility is not your responsibility. YOU know what you're saying (maybe), and THAT'S all that matters. Leave the exposition to the audience's imagination.

This is why Willis is one of the most powerful actors of this or any other era. He delivers dialogue like he's calming a jittery leopard.

Dispensing with the rug is a kenotic act of distillation. Such men eschew ornament and ostentation. Their very being seems to say, 'Have you any idea how quickly I can shower?'

It is interesting to note that *View from the Top* contains no 'powerful men'. Reduced to a few rumbling glares, Sally Weston's husband is a mute totem of masculinity, but the only man we meet in a position of authority is Mike Myers's John Witney. A man of indeterminate hair height and diverging eyeline, his physical imperfections mean that there is no way we could ever trust him.

In fact, many romantic comedies seem to be based on the theory that women are best suited to men whom, initially, they barely notice.

Paltrow is so good at being surly, one wonders whether the aspirational pep with which she is now associated is a corrective for a disposition that might be more naturally melancholic. Perhaps there are two Gwyneth Paltrows, just as there are in the film *Sliding Doors*.

For those who are less cine-literate than one would hope, *Sliding Doors* is a 1998 dramedy, written and directed by Peter Howitt, who would go on to make a film that is actually called *Dangerous Parking*. *Sliding Doors'* narrative alternates between two timelines, which diverge when the main character, Helen Quilley (Gwyneth Paltrow), runs to catch the tube.

Timeline 1: After Helen Quilley is fired from her PR job, she catches the tube, arrives home, sees her boyfriend betray her, meets a garrulous Scot (John Hannah), falls in love, wrongly accuses him of betraying her, reconciles with the garrulous Scot in rain so heavy they look like a pair of salmon trying to make it upstream, wanders into the road for no real reason, is hit by a van and dies in the hospital immediately after the garrulous Scot promises to make her very happy. Perhaps envisaging a future in which she would never get a word in edgeways was the final death blow.

Timeline 2: After Helen Quilley is fired from her PR job, she misses the tube, hits her head on a tree, doesn't find out her boyfriend is cheating on her until much later despite ample evidence, falls down some stairs, wakes up in hospital, dumps the boyfriend and meets a garrulous Scot (John Hannah) in the lift on her way out. He's on her like a duck on a June bug.

Sliding Doors is a film that asks us to have sympathy for someone who works in PR, and shows that whether you catch the tube or not, you will never get away from John Hannah. It also shows Paltrow's ability to successfully inhabit two different haircuts. It is a film which helps us remember modes of behaviour in nineties cinema that young people might now find hard to believe:

1. People once thought bright lime was an acceptable colour for a shirt.
2. People deliberately wore shirts unbuttoned, with a contrasting T-shirt underneath.
3. People listened non-ironically to Jamiroquai, and often in public.
4. Actors got out of breath from running and had centre partings even when it didn't suit them.
5. The term 'you cheating wanker' was more shocking than anything you heard on television.
6. People watched television.
7. Plot exposition consisted of debriefs with a cheeky

best-mate character in floodlight-bright, smoky pubs.*

Perhaps if *Sliding Doors* hadn't so successfully displayed Paltrow's ability to anchor a romantic dramedy, she would never have taken on *View from the Top*. We will never know because, unfortunately, there isn't a timeline in which *Sliding Doors* was never made.

* On which note, why does everyone in this film drink so much Grolsch? I've never heard *anyone* specify that they *want* to drink Grolsch. In the film, they literally talk about going out for some Grolsch. If a person were to ask for Grolsch at a bar, and for some reason they had run out of Grolsch, that person would do nothing more than shrug and accept any other beer as a more than adequate substitute. (This footnote was brought to you by Grolsch.)

How to Stay Grounded
(When You're Reaching for the Sky)

We find Donna recovering her strength, sitting in a café, looking at a fashion magazine and comparing two similar-looking yellow coats: one is high end; the other 'budget'. Her eyes drift dispiritingly to the lower-priced yellow coat, evincing doubt whether she'll even be able to afford that cheap piece of shit, when she hears a voice. The voice asks if it can take 'this' chair. We may recognise the voice, but Donna, so depressed at her limited retail opportunities, doesn't even look up. The hand connected to the voice takes hold of Donna's chair and yanks it back! Fortunately, Donna doesn't fall and sustain a serious spinal injury, but it does give her a jolt; and, what's more, it's exactly the kind of jolt she needs!

Ted, the mystery yanker, stands before Donna, his mischievous spirit and twinkle undimmed. 'Ted sure knows how to partially yank back a chair so it seems like you might fall,' Donna thinks, thoroughly revivified. Ted notes, with a wet, winning grin, that he *did* ask if he could take 'this' chair. It's a wonderful moment that speaks to the nature of consent, the dance of courtship and the need for the man to take the lead. The gasp that

Jensen emits is a gasp of surrender to the superior gender. He is the hunter, she is the quarry, and she loves it! After weeks of being surrounded by a physical wreck (John Witney) and the corrosive chromosomal conformity of her cohorts, this blast of male energy is extremely welcome. At last, someone with heterosexual balls!

Ted has enrolled at law school in Cleveland, and Donna thinks that's terrific. And do you know why he enrolled at law school in Cleveland? Because he had dinner with an amazing woman who was so set on pursuing her dreams that he felt he could too. Even though Ted has shifted into the third person, we know he's very probably still talking about Donna (but w/r/t his own dreams?).

Somewhat out of nowhere, Donna says she views Cleveland as a giant waiting room; they just have to sit out the year until their names are called so they can re-enter society. How should they occupy themselves? she coyly wonders aloud, before another one of her signature lean-ins. There is something chilling about this moment – as if the only way Donna can withstand the year is to hump her way through it. Is this what Ruffalo was referring to when he said that *Top* was originally more like a seventies sex comedy? Does Donna Jensen use the physical act of love as a way of killing time?

But before the thought grips us, we are back into montage, this time scored to Stevie Wonder's song

'For Once in My Life'.* This sequence is remarkable for resisting restrictive notions of coherence; it simply refuses to establish a pattern. In the first shot, Ted moves in to Donna's apartment; Donna bounds over, leans down and kisses him. In the second shot, we see the film *Ghost* on TV. The third shot shows Donna watching the TV. In voice-over, she talks about skies clearing unexpectedly when you were expecting a bumpy flight. While the comment contains the density of aviation imagery we've come to expect from *Top*, it doesn't quite match with the next shot: Donna wearing a heavy green face mask, a kind of goop, if you will. Donna bemoans their conflicting schedules: Ted is working hard, she says, while she spends her evenings at home eating pizza. The idea that Donna eats carbs is, undoubtedly, the funniest moment in the film. On my first viewing, I was so convulsed with mirth that I almost missed the diegetic doorbell.

It's Ted, in a pizza-delivery outfit. Donna leaps on him, pulling him towards the couch in a way that's compatible with a PG rating.

Where did Ted get this outfit? This is pre-Internet shopping. Did he go to the pizzeria and borrow one?

* Though again, not the original version. Maybe they wanted something fresher?

Or – and this is where the toes begin to arch towards the shins – did he source it from a 'speciality' shop? You know the type, often with a mannequin in the window wearing something shiny.

But on one of my many rewatches, I noticed something. In her voice-over, Donna says that one of the reasons she and Ted hadn't been seeing enough of one another was because of the extra job he took to pay for law school. Could this extra job be pizza delivery? I started to imagine the dialogue:

DONNA: You love pizza, don't you?
TED: Sure do. Especially when it's delivered.

Ted opens up another of box of pizza.

DONNA: Ted?
TED: [*mouth full of pizza*] Mmm-hmm?
DONNA: You know how expensive law school is?
TED: Yes.
DONNA: And you know how much pizza we're getting through?
TED: I'm ashamed.
DONNA: And every slice comes at a cost?
TED: True.
DONNA: As well as the delivery fee.
TED: And that's on top of the cost of the pizza itself.

145

DONNA: That's exactly right, Ted. It's an additional cost.

TED: I guess no one gets pizza for free, apart from pizzeria personnel. It's absolutely tearing me in two, Donna, especially given how expensive law school is, as you mentioned before.

DONNA: Well, it's odd that you should link the two, Ted, because I just now had a thought, and it's an absolute pippin.

TED: That's incredible. You just never switch off, do you, Donna? It was only Thursday before last that you had that other thought. But tell me, what's this one?

DONNA: What if you became a pizza-delivery guy?

TED: But I'm already working such long hours at law school. How will we make time for us?

DONNA: Well, given how much pizza we're already ordering to feed your insatiable addiction to crusty dough, you could spend the majority of the evening delivering pizza to this address.

TED: But that's ingenious!

DONNA: Thanks, Ted. I appreciate the approbation, but let me develop my initial proposition.

TED: I apologise unreservedly. I didn't mean to restrict your flow. Please go on.

DONNA: Let me tell you what I have in mind. I simply

order one pizza every hour over the course of the evening. I'd be buying you out. And the cost of the pizza will be more than covered by your wages!

TED: And then, when I arrive, I'll be in a pizza-boy delivery uniform, which you find erotic, don't you, Donna?

DONNA: Who doesn't? I hope you're not going to use patriarchal guilt to shame me about a healthy sexual drive, Ted.

TED: Apologies, Donna. But don't blame me, blame the prevailing culture that makes me its ideological pawn!

DONNA: Way ahead of you, Ted. If I lived fifteen years in the future, I'd start a podcast about it.

TED: And I'd listen in woke support.

DONNA: Appreciated.

TED: Appreciation acknowledged.

DONNA: So if you work for the pizzeria, not only will we get our dough on discount, we can also enact one of my fantasies, in which I misdirect the audience by looking sad while watching a movie, before some implied off-camera congress.

TED: Do you think the audience will buy it, Donna?

DONNA: Buy it? Of course they will. They're so exhausted by now they'll accept anything!

TED: Okay, let's do it!

He leans in for a kiss.

DONNA: Not yet! First, we need to get you into that
uniform . . .

TED: And what happens after the camera cuts away?

DONNA: That's liminal space, Ted.

TED: What goes on in liminal space stays in liminal
space, right?

*Donna pats her flank and makes a hand gesture akin
to a child pretending they're holding a gun . . .*

Ted does the same.

PART FIVE:

I BELIEVE I CAN FLY PARIS FIRST-CLASS* INTERNATIONAL

* What is classy? Herewith a brief cheat-sheet:

'Classy'	'Not classy'
First-class travel	Wet guffs
Seafood	Old strippers
Thousand Island dressing	Poverty
Dimmers	Electrical faults
Pot pourri	Spray-on deodorant (partic. when it 'crusts')
'Natural smells'	Most mould
Fresh lemon	Illness

Re-Routing

Donna's sex-pizza scheme has lent her a new glow, and she loves the slightly better commuter route she's flying. In front of the irrepressible Randy Jones, Donna demonstrates her delight at the fact that (finally!) she gets to do a full business-class service, incl. the opportunity to bake cookies. Jones laughs as if to say, 'I'm just trying to plough through this hell, but you're specifically indicating enjoyment.' He contrasts Donna's aptitude to his (lack of) commitment, saying that he still can't believe that she didn't outperform him on the exam. It's such a sparkling scene in its own right that one barely sees its plot function.

That's why we get a second scene right after it to consolidate its hidden message. It starts with a Barretian *gros plan* of bottled cheese being squeezed onto a cracker, before cutting to a wide two-shot showing Ted and Donna in her apartment. In the deep b/g we see the blinking multicoloured lights of a Christmas tree.

Cut to close-ups. Donna says that she might get a lawyer to look into this matter of the examination assessment. A frisson between them. Donna says perhaps Ted could help her out . . . He reminds her that he isn't a lawyer yet. Donna says words to the effect that 'yet' is very much the operative term. Ted, angled as ever, asks why Donna believes in him so much. Donna replies by saying, 'Somebody's got to.' You find a scene from the Golden Age of cinema more dazzling than this and I'll jet-wash your patio. But its fizz conceals a few matters that, on second glance, may reveal some faulty reasoning . . .

Given that Ted is enrolled at law school, how surprising is it that he will become a lawyer? I'd go so far as to say that it would be more surprising if he *didn't* become a lawyer. Also, Ted has parents who believed that he could do anything; he was getting encouragement until it came out of the poor boy's ears. Which means that Donna's statement that somebody has to believe in him is simply not the case. Not only are there people who already believe in him, there's no real *necessity* to believe in him. If anything, people believe in him too much.

Ted grabs Donna's arm and pulls her into a kiss. Ted's always grabbing and pawing Donna, to the extent that I feel he should just leave her alone and give her a little space. Maybe she doesn't want to be pawed. Why does everything have to be said in this supposedly (you now have three seconds to secure your stomachs . . .) 'sexy' way? Donna can't even ask for legal advice without it being interpreted as innuendo. Maybe Ruffalo, the embers of that early bacchanalian draft still smouldering, is trying to wrestle the scene back to its textual roots. And yet Ted is a family man, someone who represents stability and the possibility of connection. Oh, the duality of Man!

Donna fears family. She is worried about commitment and being open/vulnerable. The prologue, in which her callous carers didn't even have the decency to shelter her birthday candles from the wind, tells us all we need to know about the privations of her youth. She became hard, like a brioche left out in the sun.

But Man needs society, as does Woman.

During another emotionally forensic exchange with Randy Jones, much of this is underlined. Ted has invited Donna over for Christmas. '*Qu'est-ce que le prob?*' is very much Randy's attitude. Donna counters: w/r/t family + time, her trotters are arctic. You see, people always said that she was a no-hoper from Nevada and that she would never amount to much. If she opens her huge heart to Ted, what will become of her labours in the aviation service sector? And there, in nutshell format, is Donna's dilemma. I don't think even an on-screen caption could have put it more clearly or succinctly. It also happens to be the dilemma of the Great American Dream.

America is an immigrant country, or at least it used to be until some of the Caucasians decided to pretend that they'd always been there.* Make your mark, establish yourself and haul in the green; that's the USA way.

The greatest danger to that trajectory?

Happiness.

The American Constitution enshrines the pursuit of happiness, but the key word here is 'pursuit': it's all about the chase. It's no good having a nation filled with happy folk emitting contented sighs and settling down for another in a long line of restorative snoozes. That kind of attitude is not going to scare off the Man in the Black Pyjamas. You need military might. And for military might, you need economic power.

The great danger to the Great American Dream is a lack of productivity. If love derails that, there's instability, dependence, disaster . . . That's why all the great chaps of history have been emotionally cauterised. If such a notable found fond feelings for his fellow man rising up unbidden, he would banish them back to his treasonous breast. It's that kind of spirit that allows a man to wipe off the mob's gob and stride forth.

This is essentially the theme of *Phantom Thread*, Paul Thomas Anderson's mushroom omelette dramedy. The main cove, goes by the name of Woodcock, is obsessed with sewing, but in swoops a waitress who queers the

* Everyone's true place of origin is the ocean.

whole scheme. Will he stay on top of the dress business, or will he let this brazen interloper scupper his solipsism? Exactly the same plot as *Top*. Wouldn't surprise me if the whole thing was lifted wholesale. But *Phantom Thread* was garlanded, whereas *Top* wasn't even nominated for best screenplay. Such is the fate of Art. One man's Michelangelo is another man's Milli Vanilli.

Christmas: The View from Cleveland

The Stewart family home. A child holds a small model aeroplane. He whooshes it through the air. If Barreto sees a chance to develop the central metaphor of the narrative, he's going to take that chance and develop that central metaphor. And he's going to develop it like the dickens. The child's motion takes Barreto's camera around the room. No flashing lights in these premises. These bulbs are at a constant luminance and colour temperature: whoever sourced them is from good stock. As the boy hugs Donna in gratitude for this very on-brand gift, Ted takes a present to his grandmother. She's a handsome woman with a fine set of gnashers. Good grief, these people live a long time. When I was born, only one of my grandparents remained, and she was clinging on by her talons. Ted's grandmother looks in fine fettle: trim and with a knowing smile, the only evidence of senescence being near-deafness. But a condition that could well mean she feels isolated/ frightened is mercifully mined for laughs. Ted gives her a universal remote control – a chance for the art department to excel once more, and a nice meta-textual nod to Adam Sandler's matchless opus *Click*.*

The Stewarts all wear red jumpers. Is this a cult? Is Donna going to be sacrificed? When Ted turns to Donna and says, 'You're next,' the blood runs cold. Is this the end of the line? A shocking denouement in which these wool-wearing suburbanites drain the blood from our most-favoured heroine and sup her soul? No, the 'You're next' is another one of Ted's cheeky misdirects: he's about to give Donna a present. On repeat viewings, there is a persistence to Ted's flirting technique that crosses over from mere 'negging' into psychotic mind games. One has the feeling that were he to propose to Donna, he'd say, 'I've got bad news: I want to take care of you for the rest of your life.'**

Donna opens the package. It's a watch that has two faces, so that Donna can set it to two time zones simultaneously. Ted says that whenever a passenger asks her what the time is, she can think about him, even though the two things have nothing in common. As well as being terribly touching, this massively chunky watch can also help remind Donna that Ted isn't sure that she can reliably add or subtract single and low double-digit

* Of which more in Gordy LaSure's criminally underrated *The Grip of Film*.
** A statement that would sound an alarm for any *Sliding Doors* aficionado.

numbers. And there's more to come: a red jumper, so that she can match the rest of the Stewarts. Ted's mother pipes up: 'I got you a size medium. I hope you like it baggy.' I consider this to be one of the strangest pieces of dialogue in cinema history. Why would Ted's mother feel compelled to say this? It makes one wonder whether, earlier, Ted had given his mother this urgent injunction:

TED: Look, Ma, I know you handle all the sweater-buying round these parts, but this new girl of mine, she only wears things that are far too small for her.

TED'S MA: Nonsense, Ted. You can't wear wool unless it's loose. Tight wool can drive a person crazy. Plus, you have to allow for shrinkage.

TED: She don't care about no shrinkage, Ma. It looks like everything she's ever owned has been on a boil wash. I'm serious. She looks like she's had an unexplained growth spurt.

TED'S MA: Well, as far as I'm concerned, it's Christmas, and Christmas is not the time for restrictive garments, Ted. What's wrong with loose wool? I thought you said she was tall?

TED: She's twice my size, Ma. It's like looking up at Mount Rushmore.

TED'S MA: So she's gonna need a large.

TED: Don't you buy her no large, Ma.

TED'S MA: I'm telling ya, Ted, if this dame is as tall as you say, anything smaller's going to be ridiculous! It won't cover her belly button.

TED: That's the way she likes it, Ma.

TED'S MA: What is she, an exotic dancer?

TED: No, she's classy, Ma. She just likes to get a little air around the middle – like everyone who came to prominence in the mid-nineties. Remember back then, Ma? It was all about the midriff.

TED'S MA: You kids are crazy.

But Ted was right to be concerned. Donna will not don the jumper. She holds it up as if to say, 'Do you expect me to climb into this tent?' before putting it down.

As the scene draws to a close, someone called Greg (whether he is Ted's brother, brother-in-law or merely a legal colleague, we don't know) has positioned a camera on a stand. He sets the timer. Ted (who always calls Donna 'Jensen', as if they were roommates at military academy) tells her to get into the picture. She demurs, saying it's a family picture. But Ted runs roughshod over her and drags her into the frame. Greg, all forename, joins them. An off-camera flash: a new family portrait.

The kind of family that Donna never had.

We cut to Donna in profile. Behind her, the deep blue

of night; through a windowpane, rivulets of rain. Ever a master of mood, Barreto contrasts the warm camaraderie of the previous tableau (a hot, almost Spanish feel – blood reds, warm smiles) with an image of cool detachment. Her face is turned away. We see only one Jensen eye, and not directly.

Ted congratulates Donna on surviving her first Stewart family Christmas. Implication: she will have to survive more. To use an expression oddly absent from the narration, Ted's in it for the long haul. Donna says that she is unused to such family gatherings – one with no sudden gusts or impromptu show numbers. She confides that she never knew family could be anything other than shouting . . . But surely, we say to ourselves, *some* seasonal shouting is necessary to keep everyone on their toes. Don't the Stewarts risk ossification, becoming infected with a slightly distasteful pride in their own reasonableness?

We hear an instrumental of 'Time After Time' swell underneath the scene. Unconsciously, we associate this song with Ted and Donna parting. The last time we heard it, they were outside LuLu's, while Ted delineated the categories of kiss he was prepared to accept. At this moment, when they should be closer together than ever, it feels like they're drifting apart.

Donna's afraid of becoming emotionally grounded. Her heart is that red balloon, soaring high, out of sight into the stratosphere. And because of something to do with atmospheric pressure that I find hard to understand, it will almost certainly explode.

Christmas: A View from Ipswich

Despite what many believe, Christmas is still celebrated in Ipswich, often annually, and in much the same fashion as it is in the developed world.

Lights start to go up around the place in September, and they will stay there till the clocks go forward. Some people can afford to illuminate these lights; others save energy costs by having them blink on and off. Some, full of the futility of hope, travel to Ipswich to see the Christmas lights, unless they live closer to any other town.

But what did Christmas mean for me? As an Ipswichian, I was grateful for what I had: easy access to reasonably priced, non-branded footwear, very few hills and a sense that any smugness about one's circumstances was inappropriate.

Christmas also meant an increase in my domestic workload. I would assist my mother (a Norwegian whose principal adversary was dust) in decorating the whole house, and while doing so, she would assist me in my understanding that without protracted preparation, there can be no spontaneous fun. Before any decorating, we would give the house a Thorough Clean. The house

162

would already be clean enough to use as an operating theatre, but the suspicion remained that there might be dirt hiding beneath all that sterilised gloss. After the Thorough Clean:

1. All surfaces were covered in season-specific tablecloths.
2. The bannister would be wrapped in tinsel.
3. All door frames would be outlined in tinsel.
4. The cupboards would be used to store replacement tinsel.
5. Bowls of nuts would appear, gathering together once more the uneaten nuts from previous Christmases. (No living creature could open these nuts. They were so old that they were, by any reasonable assessment, fossils.)
6. The Christmas tree, purchased in mid-November to beat the rush, was placed in (what I still contend was) a too-small flowerpot and kept in precarious place with impacted, wet newspaper; a melange which, by the end of the holiday, would concretise into a giant pine-strewn ring.
7. Christmas Biscuits were baked. (These were like normal biscuits, but it was Christmas. Hence 'Christmas Biscuits'. You know, like 'Christmas Meat'. There was a coconut biscuit, a chocolate

biscuit, a ginger biscuit and a 'white' biscuit (composition unknown). I would say that over the Christmas period, I would eat between two and three hundred Christmas Biscuits. Each genus of Christmas Biscuit was stored in a large Tupperware box. The many layers of Christmas Biscuits were separated out with kitchen roll. The kitchen roll showed a festive tableau of Christmassy goodwill, but the grease from the biscuits would soak into the paper, giving the scenes a somewhat sullied feel; a literal blot on the season.)

8. Christmas Meringues were made. (I would probably eat between eight and twelve Christmas Meringues a day. At no point did my mum try to stop me from eating Christmas Biscuits or Christmas Meringues. If I ever finished a plate of Christmas Biscuits, she would just bring me another plate of Christmas Biscuits. If I started to feel sick from all the Christmas Meringues, she would just tell me to 'take a break', the implication being that I would obviously keep eating Christmas Meringues, I just had to rest. Often she would wake me up in the morning with a plate of Christmas Biscuits or, if I was looking bloated, a couple of Christmas Meringues.)

Throughout Christmas, I slept like a cobra, curled up, trying to break down the glucose. Even now, if I open a box of donuts, I have to tell myself not to eat all twelve.

My dad (a Nigerian whose principal adversary was levity) did not eat Christmas Biscuits/Christmas Meringues because he didn't like 'sweet stuff'. His favourite food was raw onion. I would frequently have to bring him raw onion slices as a snack, which meant I began to associate my dad's hunger with crying. I looked forward to reaching a similar state of zen, wherein I too could view my lethal breath as Other People's Problem. 'Who am I trying to impress?' he would say. Yet, ironically, his steadfast refusal to try to impress was impressive.

After the Thorough Clean, it was really just about counting down the days. There were three of us, and as far as my dad was concerned, Christmas just meant he had to eat two, possibly three meals wearing a paper hat. The rest was literal gravy. Norwegians have their main meal on Christmas Eve – roast Norwegian pork, boiled Norwegian cod and Norwegian sauerkraut (*surkål*). We were no different, except for the boiled cod, because my mum always felt cod was 'too fishy', i.e. too ontologically itself. Instead, we would have a Nigerian side dish (something made from beans that had been soaking since the introduction of the decimal system and then cooked in tin foil). My dad would cover this with dried, crushed chilli peppers. Whenever I see 'fusion' food, I wonder whether anyone would dare combine what was combined in our house. Our food was beyond fusion; it was fission.

Norwegians exchange gifts on Christmas Eve. I felt this was both a ruse to prevent me getting up early on Christmas morning and a way to blackmail me into a flurry of chores. My mother dismissed this as another of my deranged paranoiac fantasies, like how it was safe to go outside after 5 p.m. After the last of the sauerkraut had been washed down with a quenching draught of *julebrus*, we would clear the table, wipe the table, dry the table, replace the tablecloth, wipe the tablecloth, dry the tablecloth, wash the dishes, dry the dishes, put away the dishes in the cupboard, wipe the cupboard, dry the cupboard, vacuum any dust resulting from opening the cupboard, wipe the vacuum cleaner, put away the vacuum cleaner in another cupboard, wipe down and dry that cupboard, shower, dry ourselves, wash the towels, dry the towels and sit down on the freshly wiped sofa to exchange tokens of esteem. When I say 'we', I mean my mum and I. By this time, my dad would be asleep.

My mother always felt guilty that our family was so small. But I was happy. The thought of clearing up after another person was too terrifying to contemplate. Regardless, my mother would make sure that some of the presents I received would be 'from' our pets, so that it felt like I was part of a wider community. As a result, I never believed in Father Christmas, but I did believe that my pet rabbit shopped at Debenhams.

But of all my Christmas Memories, my most enduring is of a strange ornament that would hang from the architrave of the kitchen door. It was a mini-snowman (standard features: big belly, carrot nose, top hat, pipe), but below his bottom section/anus* dangled some foliage which – only now – I realise was mistletoe. I simply thought this snowman's somewhat greenish poo had frozen on exit.

But the main reason I loved this snowman was because of something else below its snowbottom: a metal chime hung within the mistletoe that tinkled beautifully when you touched the foliage. When I was a small child, I lacked the height to reach it, but I would hear it sound every time my mother went in and out of the kitchen to bake more Christmas Biscuits. And if she had to pop to the shops, or if she was out at work, I would draw up a chair, stand on my tiptoes and tinkle the chimes on my own. If anybody else had been there, if there had been

---

* What do you call the lower portion of a snowman? They don't have legs ordinarily, so is the anus underneath? Are we dealing with a being that's essentially all torso? Or are the legs implied, which would place the anus in the middle of the back?

167

any *witnesses*, they would have seen a small boy stretching upwards, to the limits of his capacity, as if to summon somebody, anybody, to hold him close.

Is Donna Jensen really so different from that little child?

A Ghost Rider in Cleveland

Cleveland airport, night. Donna is weary. We can tell because Paltrow has her character walk slightly slower and wobble from side to side. When the Royalty operations clerk (Duane King) asks how she is, she only manages an 'alright', chased with a good-humoured grimace. This isn't the go-getting Donna we've come to know. Camera pan to a stewardess sauntering by in sunglasses, her Nehru-collared uniform a tasteful soft orange. She stops in front of a large 'Employee of the Month' picture of Donna Jensen. She lowers her sunglasses from the bridge of her nose.

Reveal Christine Montgomery.

I doubt if the Bard himself could choreograph such an interplay of personae.

Contrast...

The image on the wall (Donna) – beaming, confident, an icon of success, while the shattered reality stands ten feet away.

With...

The viewer of the image: Christine the Dissembler, who purloined the coveted New York route and doth know deep down that her silk stockings should be cladding the feet of that insecure girl from Silver Springs.

Thus, Christine 'meets' a version of Donna, before re-meeting her moments later.

Christine and Ted sit on the floor of Donna's apartment. Christine holds a half-filled wine glass. Ted holds a bottle of a beer. The sofa is unoccupied. There's a part-consumed bottle of wine on a low table directly in front of the sofa. Donna enters holding a beer and sits down on the floor. What, we wonder, is wrong with this sofa?

After casually mentioning her great apartment in Manhattan and her new expensive hair colour 'that goes better with Chanel', Christine tells Ted that she would never have made it through training without Donna. The pulse begins to quicken. We are cineastes: we can duck the curvy daggers of swarthy men in eyeliner and receive a chastening open palm from a firm but fair mentor. Of course we find it hard to think of Jason Statham as a scientist or Sean Connery as a person; we simply grit the teeth and muddle through. But we have our limits. And the self-satisfaction of a plainly substandard stewardess, a woman who wouldn't know how to make a Duck Fart, let alone a Buttery Nipple, is more than we can bear. Particularly when a vision of stewardly excellence kneels at her feet, forced to hear tales of this coarse prodigal's unfathomable good fortune. Yet this vaunting hubris will be Christine's undoing.

First, she tells a story we could call 'The Story of the Oversized Musical Case'. The way Christine lays it out, she's on the New York to Chicago flight when a chap bounds up with an 'Oversized Musical Case'* and tries to stuff it into an overhead compartment. How he got through security is not explained. Our presumption that someone would have asked the man to hand in the item both at the check-in desk and again as he boarded the plane may not square with Christine's testimony, but the anecdote grips, and we await the sting in the tail.

Christine says she called on the spirit of Donna Jensen and asked herself what this attendant *sans pareil* would have done in her stead. Jensen and Stewart exchange a look. Barreto's camera is there to catch it. The stakes are dizzyingly high. Christine continues . . . She looked straight at the offending gentleman and said, 'Either you check it or you deplane.'

Donna is aghast. She says she certainly would not have said that, it being one's flight-attendantly duty to inform the 'musical case'-carrying miscreant that he had the option of buying another seat at half price, as per

---

* The suggested image of a large wind-up music box must cede to the more likely scenario that Christine is referring to a 'case containing a musical instrument'.

section 23.4 of the manual. Christine tries to wave away the awkward moment, saying that she can't be expected to remember everything. Donna, sensing blood, presses on. But it was the last question of the exam, she says; surely Christine would remember that? If you aren't on the absolute precipice of your seat by now, you've lost your adrenal glands.

Say I have to remember to do something. I will remember for a minute or two after you've told me, then events inevitably overtake. I will need a reminder so close to my actually needing to do the thing that you might be best advised to do the thing yourself. Perhaps Christine is a little like that? She had the whole manual memorised for the morning of the big test, but thereafter the manual is no more part of her cerebellum than her days at her mother's breast, unless, for some incestuous reason outside the scope of this drama, she remained on latch.

It's not just Donna who senses something's rotten in Baconland (Denmark). Sharing a sly *coup d'oeil* with his significant other, Ted asks whether Christine has any of those 'mini-pilot's wings' in her bag – his nephew has been hounding him for some. Christine, happy to oblige, empties out her handbag. Barreto's camera tracks in for a closer look, revealing:

1. A set of (clearly stolen, brand-new) headphones.
2. An eye mask still in its wrapper.
3. Multiple miniature bottles of spirits.
4. Tissues (in a small packet).
5. What looks like a mini-air freshener but could be perfume.

Now, one might not expect Christine to return her eye mask. Ditto the tissues – surplus mucus must be staunched. But the headphones are substantial and of the 'over-ear' type, and that's not on. Though how's she plugging them into her Discman (*Top* was lensed in 2001, so we find ourselves in a pre-iPod portable media landscape) without an accompanying stereo mini-jack socket adapter, I don't know.

We cut from Donna's puzzled face to a frenzied dream sequence, but unlike the baroque excesses of a Polanski or Tarkovsky, who might stick on a wide-angle lens and show you the dream, fogged with smoke and inexplicable drizzle, Barreto simply shows Donna half asleep. We know she's having some bad R.E.M. because she moves from side to side and occasionally groans. Sometimes the rapier is more effective than the blunderbuss. If Barreto can distil, then distil he will. It's like a partita by Bach. When you have mastery over one instrument, explore its full resonance; don't get some bozo to play bongos at the same time. A fevered Paltrow, a Ruffalo in repose (sleeping the sleep of emotionally absent men everywhere), and an off-screen voice repeating Sally Weston's ghostly blend of attestation and résumé ('Paris, First-Class International') are the only ingredients Barreto needs for a dauntingly deep draught of drama.

Donna is resolved.

Cut to Sally Weston's office, in which the gist is as follows:

Curtain up.

Wearing a short-sleeved purple polo-necked sweater, with matching eye shadow and a plum lip, Donna Jensen is at her wits' end. She looks at Sally, her pleading face looking for a bone, and not the kind you give your dog.

DONNA: Something just doesn't ring true, Sally. Sure, I'm doing well at the moment, I work hard and I naturally excel, but it's this test. Are we sure that this test was correctly graded? Are we absolutely sure about this? Because it's hard to believe. Could it be a computer fault? We see so many computer faults these days. Luggage is lost, bags misdirected. Perhaps something similar could have happened here?

Sally meets her gaze, but her tense jaw, softened only by a nude lip and the lightest brush of foundation, is resolved.

SALLY: No, it couldn't be a computer fault. You see, the thing is that all of those papers are hand-graded. No one is more surprised than me as to the outcome, but we can definitively eliminate the possibility of error.

We cut wide.

Sally is wearing capri pants, whose softly iridescent gun-metal hue speaks of an elegance beyond those common folk who scrap it out in the scrum of the quotidian.

DONNA: So you, Sally Weston, are telling me, Donna Jensen, that you, Sally Weston, can do nothing?

Angle on Sally Weston.

The scene plays like gangbusters.
Sally makes a call.
Moments later, Donna's test arrives via fax. To her horror, the test that comes through is not hers: the 'i's are dotted with hearts . . .!
The 'characterful' moment we witnessed towards the

end of Act I pays off masterfully here, catapulting us towards a key Act II turning point. But Barreto, our wise guide, fearful that audience members may not have remembered this detail, cuts back to the original test scene. This time, Donna's hopefulness ('New York, here I come') is savagely undercut by Barreto's camera as it sees Donna's test paper *intercepted* by Christine, who sneakily changes their respective candidate numbers! Christine's sly stroke to the bottom of the '7' in '1047' makes it a '1041', while an insouciant flick transforms her own candidate number – '1041' – into Donna's '1047'.

Rarely is the term 'cunt' appropriate for a trainee stewardess, but at this particular juncture it's hard to think of any other appropriate word. Fortunately for Christine, Donna writes '1' with a single downward stroke. If Donna had used serif – i.e. a top tick or horizontal line at the bottom – Christine might not have been able to make her amends so smoothly and elegantly. Perhaps a lesson to be taken from this iniquitous infringement is to adopt, in one's own life, a type of script that cannot be easily altered to further the nefarious aims of cunts.

Cut back to the present: Donna is shocked. What's more, she's flummoxed. She articulates the thoughts of anyone still watching: 'I can't believe it,' she says. And we believe her.

Just as the butter lover struggles to comprehend how similar to butter I Can't Believe It's Not Butter* is, Donna's senses rebel from the revelation that Christine is not her friend. I Can't Believe She's Not My Friend would be the title of the spreadable version of Donna's current feeling, were it to come in a tub. Donna trusted Christine, and she says as much. She also mentions the fact that the two of them were, in her estimation at least, and to use the current parlance, 'besties'. Donna sounds a final grace note of stupefaction: 'I can't believe she'd steal my test!' And yet Christine *has* stolen her test! We've seen it with our own eyes! The eyes of Barreto's camera!

We have all been betrayed, though few more than me, and the scene is a sickening reminder of the depravity to which humanity can sink when unchecked by the iron rod of the law.

Sally Weston's mind is now a synaptic firing range. She recalls the night she had the trainees to dinner. Something terrible happened. An appalling discourtesy. She must have repressed the memory, so deep was the cut: someone took her aeroplane soaps!

The crestfallen look in Donna's eyes tells us more than the most anguished soliloquy. Turns out Sally *does*

---

* An oil-based spread which, if refrigerated, can pass safely from one generation to the next.

begrudge someone taking seven or eight bars of novelty aeroplane soap. Now convinced that a grave injustice has been perpetrated, Sally stands up quickly and walks around her large desk, gesticulating to convey urgency. Sally wants Donna to retest, and fast. Fortunately, there's a group testing next week. If Donna does as well as Sally thinks she will, it'll be a pip to reassign her. The question is, how soon can Donna leave?

And then we realise.

Ted.

What the hell do we say to Ted?

Donna has a decision that she simply must make, and Sally Weston is not afraid to say that out loud. It's Donna's life, and Sally is careful to acknowledge that fact. She does not own Donna. These are two articulate Caucasians in a peer relationship discussing how best to plan destiny. But the decision weighs on Donna. This is what you might call a dilemma, and it will call for much eye moistening, hanging of the head and staring off into the middle distance.

As soon as Donna leaves, Sally telephones internal security and puts a 'ghost rider' on Christine: oddly paranormal nomenclature for a person who observes and reports on employee behaviour. Within seconds of screen time, the operative spies Christine loading up her hand-bag with company swag.

These scenes are handled with brutal efficiency. Barreto knows that the audience's collective heart is pounding like a jockey's balls on a saddle.

Ted, Ted, Ted, Ted, Ted, Ted.

Donna must face that marvellous man, and it's going to tear us in twain.

My Legal Career: A Painful View

I have something in common with Ted Stewart: I, too, studied law at university. And to the amazement of all who taught me, I graduated. I have, out of respect to The Law, never practised it, nor made any attempt to understand it. But my degree does mean that when people ask me what I studied at university, I have the opportunity to see how easily other people can detect shame.

I am ashamed of many things, but studying law is the only thing of which I am ashamed to degree level. Even lawyers don't study law at university. They study something that a human being might be interested in, like history or English literature, and after university, when they find out there's no money in history or English literature, take a law conversion course. I'm not saying we don't need lawyers. But that's only because I've been legally advised not to make that statement.

Even though I did not pursue further legal training, the kind that might render me employable rather than the proud possessor of a missed opportunity, I will never forget my time studying law at university, but only because I'll always remember how much time it took. Studying this subject with any efficacy was, for me, an impossibility. I had no idea that lectures would be in the morning. For the faculty to schedule lectures right in the middle of the time when I would be most asleep spoke of a malevolence that only became more pronounced as the term unfolded. I was then expected to go (voluntarily!) to the library and source law books, law books that were never there because they'd all been snaffled up by the rabid larks fresh from their dawn instruction. I was also expected to buy further law books with my own money! This was money that I could, and would, choose to invest in perishables.

I do recall, though, the kind words my director of studies said to me as I graduated. The emotion he felt at my departure must have been close to unbearable, because he was gritting his teeth, as if afraid that otherwise he would dissolve into tears. 'I have no idea how you managed to graduate,' he hissed, a proud twinkle in his eye. If he was asking me to admit that I'd cheated, he would need to provide evidence, and my feeling was, and still is, that I'd covered my tracks pretty well, if I had cheated (which I definitely hadn't!).

A weaker man might have confessed, but fortunately I was still high on the home-made memory serum that I may or may not have made in a lab on the outskirts of the city. It doesn't matter, because the lab has since been destroyed, if it even existed in the first place! I may not have read any law books at university, but I knew my rights: I'd watched a hell of a lot of *Columbo* when I wasn't attending seminars. *Columbo* taught me a lot of important things, like, 'If an eyepatch isn't for you, don't wear one,' and 'Who needs two coats?' Unfortunately, neither of those questions came up in the exam paper.

The point is, I graduated, and there's no probable cause (as yet) to strip me of the degree, unless they want a nasty fight. I'm proud of what I pretended to learn. Without that fake solid grounding in law, I might never have gone into light entertainment.

The Waiting Room Was My Life, as Opposed to Cleveland

It is a pensive Donna who waits in her apartment on her sofa, which does seems fine to sit on after all. The weight of the decision seems to push her down to the bottom of the frame. Barreto trusts the acting enough to hold the tableau for nearly seven seconds, although he does liven it up by tracking the camera towards her.

Ted enters, completely changing the energy of the scene: he's top of his law class! We can see that Donna is genuinely thrilled for him. She always felt that should he re-enter academia, he would thrive, and this news is vindication for them both. She rises to her feet, but does she want to rise still further . . .?

In a masterstroke of *mise en scène*, Barreto places Ted in the doorway. On his right, screen left, Donna's poster of the Arc de Triomphe; on his left, screen right, another revelatory piece of art direction: a clock whose face looks like the front of a plane – two propeller-bearing wings jut from the circular front; two wheels angle out below. The staging renders Ted as the unwitting barrier between Donna 'in flight' (as represented by the novelty clock) and her destination: 'Paris, First-Class International' (as represented by the Arc de Triomphe). He's also kind of blocking the door, which is annoying.

Donna tells Ted that she needs to go to Dallas today to retest . . .

Although we, the remaining audience, know all of this information from the previous scene, it's thrilling to rehear it in Ted's company, particularly as portrayed by Ruffalo. His jaw *drops* at Donna's recounting of Christine's duplicitous behaviour; he is *thrilled* to hear about the retesting, and with immediate, sensitive responsiveness suggests that they postpone any celebration of his own work-related progress until after Donna's return. Each new beat is handled with precision and nuance. It's a masterful performance, so light and deft that no awards committee would ever be brave enough to recognise it.

Then Donna delivers the killer blow: depending on how the test goes, she may not be able to return. She could be placed elsewhere, and gives New York as an example of one such placement. Ted expresses disbelief that Donna would make such an important decision alone, with no consultation. As Chandler from the sitcom *Friends* might have said, 'Could you *be* more autocratic?!'

Donna replies by reminding Ted how they had always said that Cleveland was just a big waiting room. But that isn't Ted's point, and what's more, it was Donna's aphorism! Impassioned, and underscored by a delicate piano melody reprising 'Time After Time', Ted essays clarification: 'For me, the waiting room was my life until I met you. I'm in love with you.'

However, Ted's transposition of Donna's metaphor doesn't quite *land*. Cleveland is an actual physical place, and so the analogy of it being a 'waiting room' is easier to process – and certainly more evocative – than the somewhat strained assertion that his 'life' was a waiting room. Life isn't a physical space! Ted knows that more than anyone! What is his 'life' now: a doing room?

'Now that I'm with you, my life is a doing room?' Doesn't sound too romantic now, does it, Ted?

But Donna is unable to change her 'destination'.

'I can't let somebody tell me that I've seen enough . . .' she says, after looking away and trying to make herself cry.

Donna's response is maddening: in what way has Ted even *suggested* that she's 'seen enough'! What does that even mean?! Is he recommending that she detach her retina? That she's had a surfeit of ocular input? Of course not. He, in a relatively benign way, was seeking to evaluate their communication process, suggesting that she was being unilateral – and how right he was! Donna is making Ted the problem, putting words into *his* mouth and blatantly mischaracterising him! This is the very definition of 'gas-lighting'! It is only because we have seen how hard Donna has worked to get to this point in her career that we are able to brook this savage rupture. It's a harrowing moment – so raw, so naked that it makes you want to reach into your ribcage and rip out your heart to check it's still there.

With that, Ted says, 'Okay,' and walks to a different part of the room, like a wounded stag. The camera dollies in to Donna, tears welling up either from emotion or allergies – it's unclear, so sudden is the redness in her eyes.

Ted gone, we join Donna at the wheel of her car – recalling *Top*'s many head-on driving shots of our stewardess-*sans-pareil*. But this time she is neither excited nor celebratory. Paltrow conveys much of this physically through her resigned body language, the voice-over merely adding another level of explication: 'I hated leaving Ted. Ted made me feel like I'd found home. The problem was I wasn't sure whether I wanted to be home.' But does Donna want to leave home for good or just pop out for some air? Also, is the home located in her or in Ted?* We simply don't know.

Ted dispatched, Donna aces her exam and receives a hero's send-off from John Witney, who reveals that the

* Donna's proposition:
  1. Being with Ted = feeling of being home.
  2. Home = place of discomfort.
  3. Therefore, Ted = uncomfortable feeling?

186

last person to get a score of 100 per cent was a certain John Witney (seven years ago).* It's Donna's time to claim what's rightfully hers.

A series of elegant, chaste, Barretian close-ups show Donna putting on her new uniform. Its classic fit and look hark back to the Golden Age of aviation that she and Sally Weston love so much. One thing's for certain: Donna is no longer Royalty Express! This is the kind of montage you only get when you're Paris, First-Class International!

She ascends escalators, deals with a higher class of traveller and distributes delicious-looking in-flight meals. Not even a hair-pulling, stiletto-stamping, rolling-on-the-floor set-piece fight with a vengeful Christine can mar her achievement.

But as the disgraced ex-stewardess is deplaned by two extras pretending to be security guards we wonder . . . at what cost Donna's ascent?

* But if he was as cross-eyed then as he looks now, why would Royalty Airlines allow him on the training programme in the first place? It seems absurd that they would let him complete the course and *then* tell him he's ineligible. What a waste of resources! A company that behaved like that would lose its shirt!

The Clothes Maketh (Not)
the (Wo)Man

At school, I was so obsessed with *The Catcher in the Rye* that I started to dress like Holden Caulfield. In the novel, Holden buys a red hunting hat in New York, after he loses all his goddam fencing gear on the goddam subway. I never lost all my goddam fencing gear, nor did I ever possess any goddam fencing gear, but I did resolve to get myself a red hunting hat, which Holden wears all the goddam time. It's a changed city now, but the retail opportunities in Ipswich did not seriously rival those of New York, and I remember that I had difficulty sourcing the requisite regalia. If I had wanted another pair of cheap shoes, boy was I in the right place. There was a shoe shop on every corner selling the kind of boxy white trainers that say, 'If you see me close to the swings, report me.' A few pounds could secure some slip-on, square-toed numbers that looked great with a long, pale-blue jean pooling at the ankle, or some slate-grey pointy numbers, perfect when taking a hotly contested sale to closed bids.

Finally, I found a forest-green army surplus cap that must have belonged to a soldier with an unusually small head. You could barely fit it on top of a clenched fist.

'How could this tiny soldier defend our nation?' I wondered. But that wasn't the strangest thing about it. For some reason, the very top of the hat was reversible. You could fold it over to reveal a circular red target underneath. Worn thus, it had the effect of making me look like I'd become separated from a group of paintballers and was now hopelessly lost.

The search for a suitably preppy houndstooth jacket was equally protracted. Ipswich was not even close to lousy with houndstooth jackets. Neither were Felixstowe, Gt Yarmouth or Kesgrave. I spent a lot of time in charity shops:

SHOP ASSISTANT: How long have you been paintballing?

YOUNG RICHARD: Why would you assume I paintball?

SHOP ASSISTANT: I suppose I took the red target on your cap as an indication . . .

YOUNG RICHARD: That I was a paintballer separated from the group, now hopelessly lost?

SHOP ASSISTANT: . . .

YOUNG RICHARD: Well, I'm not.

SHOP ASSISTANT: . . .

YOUNG RICHARD: I'm clearly an avid reader of post-war American literature.

I must have thought that one day, someone would approach me and say, 'Love the Holden Caulfield reference. How would you feel about becoming soulmates in a way that doesn't entail any actual emotional responsibility on your part?'

Now there are articles on how to get Holden Caulfield's 'literary look'. 'Practise a confident swagger, carry yourself well and wear a smile on your face. And don't try too hard – just have fun dressing up . . .' says designer Lorna Burt, about a character who ends up in a sanatorium.

People you haven't met are easy to idealise, but people who don't exist are even better. Once you've met someone you're faced with both the uncomfortable realisation that they're a person and the exhausting prospect of paying attention to what might be unique about them. Invented idols can be controlled.

What happens when we've long admired someone for their talent and then find out that despite the fact they excel at darts, they're socially conservative? How can we go on enjoying the way a person throws miniature arrows at some circular cork now that we diverge politically? And what if we find that people who make art can be terrible, perhaps even criminal? How do we get back the time we wasted enjoying their work before we knew that we wouldn't have enjoyed it if we'd known? Can we not get some kind of certification of sanctity before we allow ourselves to be moved? Because to be moved by something made by someone who has done something bad would mean that a bad person possesses the capacity to connect to us; that they haven't, somehow, forfeited their humanity.

So we must be on guard against gurus, lest their imperfections infect.

'What is the real Sally Weston like?' we wonder. Is Donna wise to follow in her trailblazing jet stream? Does she have feet of clay beneath her anti-deep-vein-thrombosis support socks?

PART SIX:
A RAPID DESCENT

Ladies and Gentlemen, We Have Reached Our Destination (for Now)

Donna finally flies First-Class International! To Paris! She, and our hearts, soar.

When she lands, she decides to see the city, which she does in a whirlwind of second-unit camera work, all the while wearing the yellow coat she saw in the magazine (the more expensive one? We imagine so!) and a black beret. Some might think wearing a black beret would be a little 'on the nose', not far removed from wearing a stripy top and a string of onions, but not Barreto. Barreto knows that clichés exist because they are underpinned by truth.

But it's not all Nutella crêpes and frothy coffee. There's unease.

Donna sits in a café, the Eiffel Tower in the background, and struggles to write a postcard, only getting as far as 'Dear Ted'. A promising start, but not enough on its own. On board a plane, she is hectored by a short Frenchman asking for more champagne. We see that First-Class International isn't all lobsters and steaming napkins. There's conflict, red in tooth and claw.

In order to compose herself, she glances at her watch, the two-faced gift from the one-faced Ted. The emotion threatens to fell her in the aisle. She loosens the Bollinger, but the cork flies out, striking the short wine-lover on the forehead with savage force. All she can do is say how *désolé* she is, but the damage has been done. She's screwed up. *Un-Royaltily.*

Another montage follows hot on the heels of this melee, this time in a single breathtaking motion-control shot panning round Donna's apartment. The seasons change, but Donna stays the same, apart from when she's wearing fewer clothes. Or maybe she does change, but just into different pants. Also as a person maybe? Perhaps feeling more tired overall, but still attractive? Or older, but still young-looking?

A collage of answerphone messages tells a tale of continual demands to attend work. The reality of stewardessing at the highest level is stark – you are *literally always flying.*

Donna begins to reflect . . .

1. At a party in Brooklyn, she sees her friend enjoying family life. Why isn't *she* enjoying family life?
2. While on a Christmas Eve flight, Donna sees a newspaper clipping showing a picture of Ted Stewart. He has been hired by a local law firm.*

---

* One might ask whether this would be of sufficient public interest to

196

Why hasn't *she* been hired by a local law firm?
Or failing that, why isn't she holding the non-
newspaper-clipping version of Ted, i.e. Ted himself
(the actual Ted)?

3. When she lands in Paris on Christmas Eve, she
sees couples strolling arm in arm. Why isn't *she*
strolling arm in arm (with another person)?

4. She sees further happy families. Why has there
been no further development w/r/t her question
outlined in point 1?

5. She sees a couple aggressively necking in the street,
but she's too mournful to enjoy watching them.
Why isn't anyone forcefully exploring *her* mouth?

6. She walks alone, merely looking elegant, ignored
by everyone. Apart from the fact that the director
told them to, why is everyone ignoring her?

7. She stares at a roaring fire, but she is not at
hearth and home; the roaring fire is an image on
a television in a sterile hotel room and lacks the
directional, frontal heat she craves. She clutches the
jumper that Ted's family gave her, but which she
still won't wear on account of it being too shapeless.
Why isn't *she* in front of a non-meta heat source?

---

appear in printed form. A minor quibble, but we've come to expect so
much from *Top* that any expediency in exposition stands out.

This montage suggests, gently and without didacticism, that Donna might need even more than Paris, First-Class International.

Christmas in Paris should be a dream. But, the film courageously asserts, dreams are not reality. We can't live in dreams any more that we can live in the clouds or under socialism. At some stage, you have to touch down. Although not explicitly Judaeo-Christian in emphasis, the film can't help but evoke Mark 8:36: 'For what shall it profit a man, if he shall gain the whole world and lose his own soul?' Bit of a leading question, but you catch JC's drift.

It is only when Donna bumps into Sally Weston at the airport that she's able to confront her loneliness. She confides to Sally that she misses Ted. When Sally questions why Donna left him, Donna invokes Sally's book. Sally politely demurs, suggesting that perhaps she has not read it carefully enough. She quotes her own text, an act that might seem obnoxious and grandiose in a less well-drawn character: 'Every pilot needs a co-pilot. It's awfully nice to have someone sit beside you. Especially when you hit some bumpy air.'

It always strikes me as curious that Sally doesn't use the term 'turbulence' here, especially as it's one of the few times this particular aeronautical term could be employed both accurately and conversationally. In fact, no one really says 'bumpy air'.* 'Bumpy air' sounds like how you would describe turbulence to a toddler. Also, Donna could be forgiven for feeling that Sally *was* encouraging her to focus on her career. Sally explicitly asked Donna to follow her 'head, not her heart'. Was this something likely to upbuild and encourage the relationship between Ted and Donna? In fact, Sally's inability to see her own role in Donna's present situation is borderline psychotic.

Movingly, though, she offers to take over Donna's shift, perhaps in response to the first pang of conscience that she, Sally Weston, has ever felt in her life.

* Maybe because Co-Pilot Steve used the term 'turbulence' in an earlier scene, they thought that to use it again here would be repetitive? Plausible, esp. seeing as *Top* yearns to make each moment fresh and bespoke.

'Window Seat or Aisle?' Can You Sit in Both at the Same Time?

Alain Badiou, the post-Marxist continental philosopher, talks of the incommensurability of certain modes of thought, often citing the death of Archimedes as an example. The basic gist runs thus:

> *The Death of Archimedes – A Short Sketch*
> A Roman general, Marcellus, sends a soldier to fetch esteemed thinker Archimedes, but the Byzantine brainiac is working on a mathematical problem and ignores the soldier's summons. Not unpeeved, the squaddie restates his case, i.e. up you get. Archimedes, without looking up, says he'll come when he's solved the problem, thank you very much. The military man, exasperated and angry, kills Archimedes.

Badiou terms this a 'philosophical situation'. Archimedes' exercise in pure reason is not compatible with the civic demand made on him by the state; they have different temporality. The former conforms only to its own rhythm; the latter demands urgency. There is no crossover, and the only way to breach the gap between them is by the use of violence. This is why there are so many fist fights at the EasyJet customer service counter.

How can Donna Jensen square her desire for Paris, First-Class International with her desire for home and hearth (as embodied in Ted Stewart) without doing violence to her heart?

We all know the path to success requires that dead wood be burnt. And by dead wood, I mean living people. Only when you've established your dominion can you reward yourself with romance. You cannot dedicate yourself to self-advancement when you're in a relationship: how can you help yourself and another person at the same time? It's impossible. Here's a *Times* obituary you'll never read: 'As great a rock star as he was, he was perhaps an even greater husband.' No one who achieved anything was 'there' for someone else. They were elsewhere. Achieving.

In this respect, romantic comedies have much less moral integrity than violent action films. The vigilante remains an outsider. He is not rewarded. He remains poor, unmoored, lonely. Contrast that with the couple, whose highest priority is each other. How are they meant to stop the Kurdish terrorist from releasing the nerve gas? They'd be too busy staring into each other's eyes to notice; and if they *did* notice, how would they form a coherent plan under pressure, while respecting each other's equally valuable personhood?

201

The only dilemma in the romantic comedy is: what keeps the couple apart? Once they're together, that's the end of anything interesting that could be said about them. It's a quick fade to black and then on with their inward-facing existence. Two people whose highest priority is each other is not a monetisable prospect; nor does conscientious mutual consideration make for movie magic.

In the romantic comedy, a man, let's call him Brad, neglects his family for his career, with the inevitable estrangement that follows, only to realise, late in the third act, that his family comes before everything. At this point, Brad will reject his work, refuse to give the Big Presentation to Yamamoto Corp. and run like hell to Bobby's piano recital, and when he arrives he'll cheer louder than all the stiffs who wasted their time attending previous school events, because this school event is actually the important one and makes up for all the other (historic) absences, so who cares if his suit is sweat-sodden and he paid $20,000 for a seat on the last plane back from Denver, because when Brad hugs his child, who played piano better than he ever thought possible because his awesome dad showed up for him, a seemingly innocuous remark from a bystander triggers one of Brad's madcap ideas.

And they all run – as a family – into the patrician office of Brad's Boss, disrupting its *froideur*, and Brad outlines an idea of such brilliance that the secretaries who've been there since Brad was a trainee stand up and start applauding – and Brad's Boss gets a faraway look in his eye – like this might work – perhaps this is the very thing our business needs to survive in the modern competitive landscape – even though his yuppie son Bobby says, 'Brad's crazy – Brad's always been crazy – it'll never work – don't tell me you *like* this crazy idea' – to which Brad's Boss says, 'What do you know? – You've had a silver spoon up your ass for so long it's scooped out your brains – and Bobby looks shocked because an adult said something about a spoon going up someone's ass – but it's okay – it's just salty talk – in fact, it shows healthy non-conformity – and Brad's Boss looks at young Bobby and says, 'You know what, son? I had a crazy idea once: it was about setting up a company that takes risks. And that company put us on the map, only now I think we've lost our way, and maybe that's because we've forgotten how to be crazy. And sure, maybe your dad *is* kinda crazy, but if Brad's crazy, so am I. We could all use a little crazy right now' – and then Brad's Boss looks up at Brad and asks, 'Will you come back and maybe run the company for me? I think it's time I took the silver spoon out of my own ass and used it to make a little hay while the sun's still shining' – and now Brad and his wife are hugging and bringing Bobby in close – so close – they've never been this close – or rich – they're richer than ever

– but truer too – and they'll never forget what's important – and although it may look like they're having their
cake and eating it – for some reason it's different from
having your cake and eating it – it's more like working
out how to manufacture cake on such a scale that you
couldn't eat it all if you tried.

But people who make films that tell us to prioritise
family over work still expect us to pay to see their films.
If I were to try to see one of their exhortations at the cinema, but found myself impecunious, could I, as a lover
of romantic comedies, appeal to the good heart of the
usher?

AYOADE: Don't you see? I *know* I don't have any
money to pay for a ticket. That's because I spend
so much time playing with my children and being
present to those I love. I've been fired from every job
I ever had, but my school-concert attendance record
is second to none. They actually wondered whether
I was a talent scout, but I said, 'No. I'm not a talent
scout. I was a talent scout, but they kept wanting me
to scout talent instead of impulsively fly kites with
my children and giddily run through meadows and
show up at my wife's work (she's a surgeon) and
say, "Come with me now, I miss you. What's more
important, this emergency appendectomy you're

performing or taking time out for cupcakes and waffles?"' I've followed the making of [insert name of film] for a long time. I managed to read the script of [insert name of film] in advance – you see, I used to be an actor for a while – I was actually asked to read for a part in [insert name of film], but I'd promised my niece I'd play Poohsticks with her whenever she wanted, and she said she wanted to play Poohsticks at the same time as the audition, and she lives in Peckham, so it involved taking a train out to the country to find a stream that was magical enough. So I was – big deal – three or four days late for the audition. But those precious moments trudging through the pissing rain trying to find a stream that precisely conformed to a half-remembered line drawing of a stream from a book that I forgot to bring in the heady rush of it all . . . well, those are moments you never get back. Anyway, I was so impressed with the script of [insert name of film] and its message of family first that I thought I'd visit the set and tell the director how proud I was that he would devote so much of his time and effort to it, and that even though I wouldn't get to play a part in [insert name of film] because of my own family commitments, I was just so glad, as a cinema fan, that it was going to be made.

So I went to the set, but I was told I couldn't see the director and that I had 'no right to be there'.

So I said, 'Fine. I'll wait.'

And they said, 'Well, we can't stop you.'

And I said, 'That's right. You can't stop me.'

And then, later, I said, 'Because you don't own the road, do you?'

Which was both true and something I hadn't thought of straight away. In fact, there was a big enough gap between the two statements that I had to remind the guard what I was originally talking about.

I waited until the director was finished for the day, which was very late, and I was sad because I actually missed dinner with my family. I was about to check into a Travelodge when I saw the director leaving the studio, so I ran up to him and said, 'I just want to say thank you for making this film about how important family is, because it's very important to me.' And he said, 'Who are you?' And I said, 'A family man.'

And he said that being a family man was the best thing you could be, and that he had a family himself.

'I expect you'll be going home to see them now,' I said.

He said that he wished he were, but they lived in America. He had two daughters. (His wife had been accidentally decapitated at a theme park, but now they had a really good live-in au pair.)

I said, 'Why don't they come over to be with you?'

He said that he works such long hours that he wouldn't get to see them anyway, and that even though it was hard for him to be away all this time because he's such a committed family man, they all decided it was best if they stayed in America with the au pair – he couldn't stress enough how good this au pair was – but he would get to see them in five weeks' time.

I said, 'Why don't they come to the set? They could shout out ideas and create a nice atmosphere for everyone.'

He said, 'It's a nice thought, but I need to concentrate, and I don't know that I could do that with them around.'

I said, 'So you would rather they weren't here?'

There was a pause. He seemed tense for some reason. So I decided to ask another question to relax him.

'What scene were you shooting today?' I asked.

'The scene where the hero's wife says that if he can't make it to their son's softball final, he needn't bother coming back.'

'I like that scene,' I said.

'So do I,' he said.

We both bowed our heads a little.

'Are you going to be here all night?' interrupted the guard. 'Some of us have got homes to go to!'

'We're talking about the importance of family, asshole,' I explained.

The guard said something about not having seen his kids for two weeks now because he'd been working so late, and I said he should be grateful for the overtime and that there were plenty of people who would kill for his job.

The guard said, 'Don't you see the irony?'

I said that I didn't. And that if there were any irony about the place, I would have seen it because I'm an artist, and that's what I'm trained to do. I said that the director and I were creative people, and that we had a different ontology to him. 'Our needs are non-commensurate with yours, Marcellus . . .' I added.

'Don't proof-quote Alain Badiou to me,' said the guard. 'I haven't got the time.'

We looked at each other. We saw one another. We, finally, understood one another.

We all laughed and held each other close.

I'd never felt as close to anyone as to those two men. All three of us, desperate to get back to our families, but instead deciding to go out for ribs, and talk about the breakthrough we'd made, and also to drink beer. Somehow we all lost our phones so we couldn't get Ubers, and I decided to walk because it wasn't that far, but I realised it was at least fifty miles till I would be outside my front door. And then I thought, 'I wish we could get an au pair. I'm a hostage in my own home.'

The usher looked at me. I could tell my story had moved her. She now knew there was more to this world than the mere material. That something as tawdry and gross as money would be a Badiou-like barrier to our two souls touching in a subconscious fist-bump of empathy and understanding.

But by that time the film was nearly over. I think that's why she told me to leave.

Emergency Landing

Donna figuratively and literally flies to Ted's family home. Her taxi pulls up outside its grand exterior. She rings the bell. No answer. A lesser stewardess would have drawn stumps for the day, headed back to the pavilion and surmised that this reconciliation was just not meant to be. Not Donna Jensen. She has the tenacity of a mountain goat.

With the boldness only low BMI can bring, she opens the door (technically trespass) to find . . . Ted's grandmother. Donna confides in her. She confesses that she messed up . . . She thought Paris, First-Class International would make her happy . . . but it didn't. Ted makes her happy. In short, she bloody loves Ted. She tries to cry for a short while, but nothing comes. Then, a thought that triggers a rueful smile: 'You haven't heard a single word I've said, have you?' The deft seeding of this ancient woman's near-deafness pays the kind of dramatic dividends for which Arthur Miller would have killed.

'I did,' Ted says, descending the stairs.

How apposite that Donna should meet Ted on the stairs, a place of transition! Ted is neither 'on ground level' nor 'in the stratosphere', he is 'on the stairs'. In this moment he represents a third way. A life that can balance career and family. A synthesis. Donna reiterates both her love and her willingness to be Cleveland-based. He asks her how on earth could any woman be happy in Cleveland? 'Because you're in Cleveland,' she fires back, like the loveliest machine gun in the world. Is there anything more romantic than someone's willingness to remain in a place that is demonstrably unsatisfactory?

Donna bends down to kiss Ted, the camera tracks back, and we hear Donna's final assessment of her journey: 'Life is a series of arrivals and departures. But I learnt there is more than one way to spread your wings.'

As if to answer the question 'How, exactly?' we join Donna in the cockpit of an aeroplane. Her new role?

Pilot.

She turns and winks to camera.*

Why or how or when she became a pilot is not the concern of the film at this point, nor is it a concern of ours. The film has 'flown' by and we're 'thrust' into an artfully edited bloopers reel, capped off by an extended dance routine to the song 'We Are Family', but with the world 'family' replaced by 'royalty' – a sly reference to Royalty Airlines. Eerily, Donna is dancing with Christine, who by this point has been unmasked as a

---

* Echoes of Haneke's *Funny Games*?

211

liar and a thief. When we last saw these two characters, they were literally *wrestling on the floor* in an unbending attitude of mutual recrimination. To see them thus reunited is quite shocking – like a more celebratory iteration of John Travolta's 'temporal resurrection' at the end of Quentin Tarantino's laboured *Pulp Fiction*. But maybe we're watching not Donna and Christine, but the actresses Gwyneth Paltrow and Christina Applegate? Could this be a Godardian moment of extra-narrative exuberance? It is tempting to speculate, but only Barreto and his gifted creative team know the answer to that one!

All we know is that something we never thought possible has occurred.

The film ends.

The Charred Wings of Icarus, on a Bed of Humble Pie

In Greek myth, Icarus's father, Daedalus, is a master craftsman whose previous credits include the Labyrinth (the pre-Bowie version). Like many men, he and his son have a pressing need to get out of Crete, so Daedalus, with only a tub of wax and a fistful of feathers, makes them a pair of wings each.

Bosh.

Daedalus is up in the firmament, loving life. But – and this is crucial – with a caution regarding altitude-to-heat ratios that only maturity can bring.

Different story with his nipper.

Flushed with the excitement of early aerodynamics, Icarus ignores his father's warnings to pull up from the life-giving orb.

Wallop.

Man's wax gets warm and the young pup plops into the drink.

Stanley Kubrick once said, 'I've never been certain whether the moral of the Icarus story should only be, as is generally accepted, "Don't try to fly too high," or whether it might also be thought of as "Forget the wax

213

and feathers, and do a better job on the wings.""

Paltrow's Donna Jensen is the twenty-first-century Icarus of whom Kubrick dreamt. She could probably fly right *through* the sun if she wanted!

We applaud both her dogged grit and the film's message: that there are some people who, despite shutting everyone out of their lives in order to achieve their goals, can repair the untold damage they've wreaked by making a small admission of culpability late in Act III, followed by a declaration of love.

Along the way, Donna has 'jettisoned' the unwelcome 'cargo' of false friends, useless parents and an inconstant lover, metabolised the wisdom of an elder (Sally Weston) and created a robustly individualistic self-actualised existence with the renewed, unflinching support of Ted Stewart, who will keep her 'grounded' on the solid soil of Cleveland should she ever 'fly' too high.

Knowing this, we, the audience, refreshed from this peerless 'in-flight' entertainment, can recharter our own journeys, arrive at the destination of our heart's desire and, once we've come safely to a stop, command our *own* 'view', from the Top.

Clearing the Cabin: What Makes *View from the Top* a Modern Masterpiece?

The aim of this book has been to ask that very question, and then really drag out the answer. In considering whether any movie could be classed as 'a modern masterpiece', Team Ayoade asks itself the following questions:

Is it timeless?
Is it urgent?
Is it mysterious?
Is it prophetic?
Is there a training montage?

Then, after a rest/snack:

Does it exhilarate?
Does it provoke?
Does it instil a sense of the infinite?
Does it confirm what you already thought?

And once I'm in pyjamas, all cosy, with face squeaky clean:

Can it comfort me in the dark?
Is it readily available?
How long is it?

If the answer to any of these is 'maybe' or 'less than ninety minutes', the film makes it through to the next round, the rules of which remain unclear. Two increasingly abstract stages follow, climaxing in a secret, subconscious ballot, from which I frequently abstain. When I wake up, I transcribe whatever markings are left on my body.

Top, like Donna Jensen in the seminal Second Royalty Airlines Examination Scene, got the maximum score.

Top is the film of my life.

Top goes deep within me.

To get to the bottom of me, you have to get to the bottom of *Top*. Two bottoms, same shit.

When I pitched the idea for this book, my nameless publisher Walter started to cry. And not just because he was tired. It was also because he was sad. It *felt* like he kept using the word 'betrayal', but I couldn't be sure because I was scrolling through my mental Rolodex of other publishers who might be interested in the book and who didn't look so goddam *mournful* about its 'non-existent commercial potential'.

'How are we meant to sell a book about a film no one has seen?' he sobbed, in the first of a series of coded attacks on my masculinity.

Duh . . . The whole *point* of the book is to restore the film to the canon. If everyone knew about *Top*, why would I be utilising my hard-won clout within the entertainment industry to change hearts and minds?

Also, why would he use the word 'betrayal' in relation to me? That word couldn't apply to me *less*. How would I *let someone down*? That's impossible. I've been *super-present* to everyone I've ever met and have always acted in the best interests of everyone else around me. In fact, I've been *beyond* selfless. Selfless to such an extent that you could say it's damaging. To the extent that people might say, 'Richard, hold up a moment. Can you stop caring so frickin' much? You're going to die from all the giving. There's only so much empathy a person can emit before becoming a husk. You're wrung out! There's going to be nothing left of you. Where are *you* in all this serial magnanimity? Are you just a membrane through which the hopes, desires, needs and fluids of everyone else in the world can pass?'

Why wouldn't my nameless publisher Walter want me to be my best self? My most truthful self? Why was he trying to hurt me? Was he an enemy sent to destroy me? Would he try to strangle me if he stopped cowering?

Wouldn't it be better to hold him down by sitting on his chest until I could be sure?

And then I laid it out straight.

'I'm gonna write a monograph on *View from the Top*, see? And I'm going to interweave my response to this little-seen gem with moments and memories from my life. And there ain't nuttin' you or any of you dirty heels at Faber can do, see? Cos I ain't doing some picture book called *Cats Who Love Without Boundaries* or whatever the hell else is de rigueur with you douchebags down in Soho Town. I'm writing a book for *me*, you rat. You hear me? This is for *me*, you low-down louse. Ya hear? For me, Ma, ME!!!'

'No one liked your last book, but at least it had variety! At least there were *different* things to dislike!' wheezed the stricken wretch. 'Also, why are you calling me Ma and trying to climb on top of me?'

'Not my problem, Ma,' I retorted, never shy to use the same tort twice. 'Let me do my job, i.e. change literature for ever, and then you can do your job, Ma!'

'I refuse to breastfeed you.' The crack of a rib.

'I don't want your titty milk, Ma. All I want is that you make everyone in the English-speaking world buy at least one copy of . . .'

And then I realised I didn't have a title yet.

I started to laugh. Slowly at first, then faster, then at

medium pace, then I paused for a while before getting right back into it.

Ha! Ha! Ha! Ha! Ha! Ha!

It was so simple.

Question: where was I?

Answer: on top.

Question: who was I?

Answer: Ayoade.

Note to director: *Ayoade looks up. Camera moves in to capture this revelatory thought.*

Ma was asleep now, but her promise was alive.

And so was/is this book.

Ayoade on Top.

My modest aim is that it delights, entertains and reconfigures the relationship between you and the universe.

I hope you have the humility to receive it.

Suggested Further Viewing

Air Marshal (2003; dir: Jakubowicz)
Airport (1970; dir: Seaton/Hathaway)
Baggage Claim (2013; dir: Talbert)
Collision Course (2012; dir: Ray)
Executive Decision (1996; dir: Baird)
Fly Away Home (1996; dir: Ballard)
Flyboys (2006; dir: Bill)
Ground Control (1998; dir: Howard)
High Life, The (TV series)
Hijacked (2012; dir: Nutt)
I'm So Excited (2013; dir: Almodóvar)
Pan-Am (TV series)
Sky Captain and the World of Tomorrow (2004; dir: Conran)
Sky Kids (2008; dir: DeVilliers)
Snakes on a Plane (2006; dir: Ellis)
Soul Plane (2004; dir: Terrero)
Turbulence (1997; dir: Butler)

Team Ayoade hopes this book leads to a revival of aeroplane-centric dramedy. We need more stories about cabin crew, pilots and ground staff, and we need new voices to tell them.

We hope to fly with you again.

Index